CAMBRIDGE
UNIVERSITY PRESS

CAMBRIDGE
Primary Science

Learner's Book 3

Jon Board & Alan Cross

CAMBRIDGE
UNIVERSITY PRESS

University Printing House, Cambridge CB2 8BS, United Kingdom

One Liberty Plaza, 20th Floor, New York, NY 10006, USA

477 Williamstown Road, Port Melbourne, VIC 3207, Australia

314–321, 3rd Floor, Plot 3, Splendor Forum, Jasola District Centre,
New Delhi – 110025, India

103 Penang Road, #05–06/07, Visioncrest Commercial, Singapore 238467

Cambridge University Press is part of the University of Cambridge.

It furthers the University's mission by disseminating knowledge in the pursuit of
education, learning and research at the highest international levels of excellence.

www.cambridge.org
Information on this title: www.cambridge.org/9781108742764

© Cambridge University Press 2021

First published 2014
Second edition 2021

20 19 18 17 16 15 14 13 12 11 10 9 8 7 6 5 4 3

Printed in Italy by Rotolito S.p.A.

A catalogue record for this publication is available from the British Library

9781108742764 Paperback with Digital Access (1 Year)
9781108972574 Digital Learner's Book (1 Year)
9781108972581 eBook

Introduction

Welcome to Stage 3 of Cambridge Primary Science. We hope that you enjoy these exciting activities at Stage 3. At Stages 1 and 2 you learned a lot about the world and about how to be a scientist. This year you will learn even more!

An important part of Stage 3 is that you will learn how to do five different types of science investigations:

- research
- fair testing
- observing over time
- identifying and classifying
- pattern seeking.

These types of investigations will make you an even better scientist and will help you learn much more about the world.

At Stage 3 you are going to learn about:

- plants
- materials
- light
- living things
- forces
- the Earth in space.

You will learn new things and new words so it will help to talk about your science. Make sure you talk with your classmates as well as your teacher and other people.

You may find when learning science that some things feel easy but others are harder. You may sometimes get things wrong. Do not worry about this. As learners we don't get things right every time. But this can help us to learn. Some scientists have found that we may learn even more when we get a few things wrong. This is because it makes us think harder about what we are learning. So, remember, enjoy your science but be ready to talk about it and think hard!

Jon Board and Alan Cross

Contents

Contents

How to use this book

In this book you will find lots of different features to help your learning.

What you will learn in
the unit. ────────→

We are going to:
- learn about mixtures and how to separate them
- observe the properties of materials in mixtures

Questions to find out what
you know already. ────────→

Getting started

These beans are all mixed together.
- Tell a friend how you would separate the beans into the different types. What could you use to help?
- Draw diagrams to show your ideas.

Important words and
their meaning ────────→

conditions   germination
seedling   shoot   wilt

A fun activity about the Science
you are learning. ────────→

Activity 2

Make a model plant

You will need: paper, card, a straw, string, glue, sticky tape

Making a model will help you learn about plants. You can touch the model and observe its parts.

Use the materials to make a model plant with a flower, stem, leaves and roots. Label your model.

An investigation to carry out
with a partner or in groups. →

Think like a scientist 2

Questions about friction

You will need: a forcemeter, some masses, some water, some shoes or other objects to pull

Zara and Arun have a new question about friction. What type of scientific enquiry can they do to find out the answer: research, pattern seeking, observing changes over time, fair testing or identification and classification?

Questions to help you think about how you learn.

How did the practical work help you to learn today?

This is what you have learned in the unit.

Look what I can do!

- ☐ I can name two materials that dissolve in water and one that does not.
- ☐ I can ask a scientific question and plan the right type of scientific enquiry to find the answer.
- ☐ I can record my observations in tables and diagrams.
- ☐ I can explain how to stay safe in an investigation.

Questions that cover what you have learned in the unit. If you can answer these, you are ready to move on to the next unit.

Check your progress

Talk about these questions.

1 Complete these sentences. You can use these words.

not alive | can have young | cannot have young | alive

I know this eagle is _____ because it _____

I know this candle is _____ because it _____

At the end of each unit, there is a project for you to carry out, using what you have learned. You might make something or solve a problem.

Project: How do plants use water?

Make a zig-zag book explaining the journey of water through a flowering plant.

A zig-zag book is like a 'fold up' poster. You need to draw and write to explain how water:

- is in the soil,
- is absorbed by the roots,
- moves up the stems,
- is used in leaves and flowers.

Start by researching in books and on the internet. Then write and draw diagrams to explain what happens to water in a plant.

Use arrows to show how the water moves in the plant.

Open the book to watch the poster grow!

My story of the journey of water through a plant

some water leaves each leaf

in each leaf water + air are used

water travels up the plant in the stem

water ab...

Working like a scientist

Different types of science enquiry

At Stage 3 and during the later stages of Cambridge Primary Science you will carry out five kinds of science enquiry. These allow you to think and work scientifically.

classifying
fair testing
identifying
pattern seeking
research
science enquiry

Research

In science you can answer your questions by finding information in books, on the internet and from videos.

Sofia is doing research on plants.

Fair testing

Fair testing allows you to see how changing just one thing affects something else. You change one thing then observe or measure what happens to the other thing. You must keep all the other things the same.

> In my fair test I changed the plastic only. I observed only how it blocked the light. I kept everything else the same.

> This is the best plastic for sunglasses.

Observing over time

You can answer some science questions by observing over time.

By observing seeds grown with different amounts of water Sofia can answer this question: How does the amount of water affect the growth of plants?

Sofia is observing the effect of watering over time.

NO WATER

WATER EVERY 3 DAYS

WATER EVERY DAY

Pattern seeking

As scientists you will look for patterns as these can help you to find out more. We call this pattern seeking.

Can you see a pattern in this shell?

We also look for patterns in our results. Patterns in results can be very useful. They help us to predict what may happen in the future.

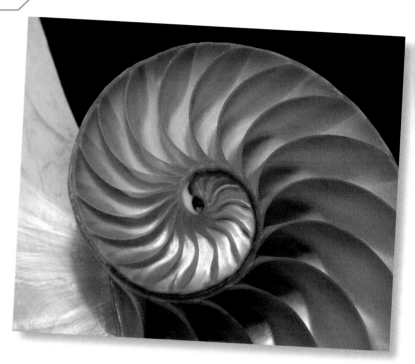

In this bar chart we see the water level in a glass of water which holds plant stems. We can see the level going down from day one to day five.

What might the level be on day 6?

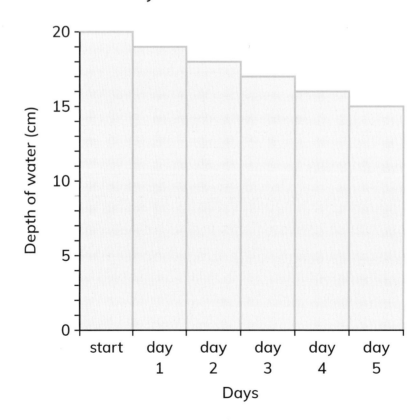

Identifying and classifying

When you work as a scientist it is important to identify different things such as: materials, plants, animals, and parts of the body.

One way that scientists learn about these things is to put them into groups, and this is called classifying. Here we can see that materials have been sorted into two groups. These groups are magnetic materials and materials that are not magnetic.

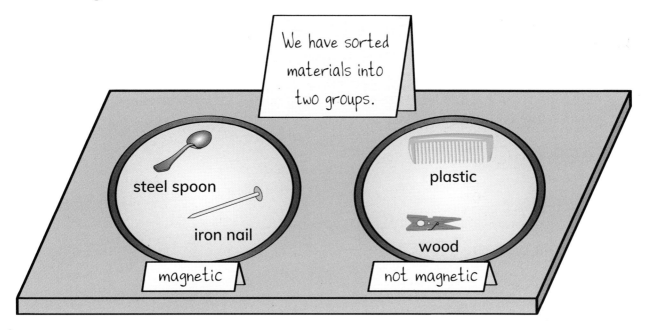

Questions

1 Have you done any of these things in the past?

2 Which type of science enquiry would you most like to do? Why?

3 Which type of science enquiry do you think is the most important for scientists?

Plants are living things

> ## 1.1 Alive or not alive?

We are going to:

- find differences between things that are living, were once alive and that have never lived
- use seven rules to see if something is alive or not
- learn about scientific enquiry
- learn how to classify things
- collect and record observations.

Getting started

Look at the picture.

- How can we know that something is alive?
- Which things are alive?
- Which things have never been alive?

dead   gas   oxygen
seeds   waste product

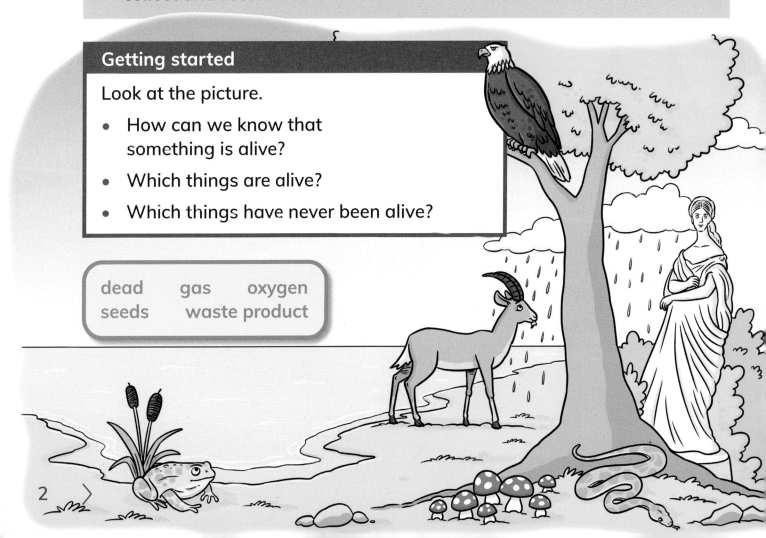

Plants grow

This young plant has just started growing.
It needs water and sunlight. The young plant
can feel light and it grows towards the light.

The young plant is alive.

The plant makes the gas called oxygen.

Oxygen is a waste product of plants. Plants
get rid of oxygen into the air. Oxygen is one
of the gases in the air.

The oxygen in air is very important
because it is a gas which all
animals need to live.

When the plant is older it will make
seeds. New plants will grow from
the seeds.

Questions

1 Are all plants and animals alive?

2 Is every part of a plant alive?

3 How could we care for a plant that
   is growing in the classroom?

Seven rules: alive or not alive?

Each day you see animals and plants that are alive. You also see materials like wood and straw that were once part of a living thing. Other materials, like sand, have never been alive.

Try using these seven rules to see if something is alive. Living things do all seven!

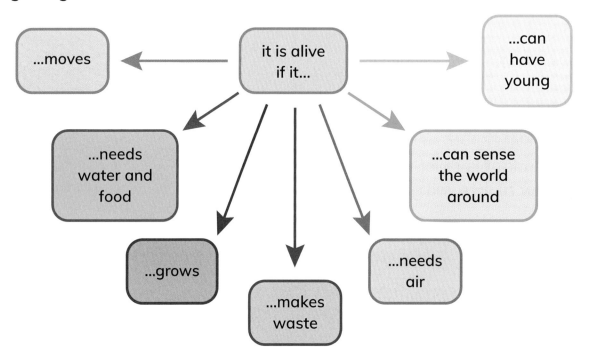

Think like a scientist 1

Alive or not?

You will need: a plant, a bare branch, a plastic plant, a block of wood, a piece of rock

With a friend talk about these things. Describe each one. What is it made of? Where did it come from?

Is it alive or not alive? Use the seven rules to help you.

Continued

Record what you think in
a table.

This was a science enquiry
because you were identifying
and classifying things.

Object	What is it made of?	Is it alive or not alive?
A rock	rock	not alive

How am I doing?

Show other people your table. Do they agree with you?

Think like a scientist 2

Alive, once alive or never alive?

You will need: access to the school grounds, pencil

Look around the classroom and in the school grounds.
Copy and complete this table to record things that:

• are alive now   • have never been alive.

• were once alive

The seven rules will help you.

Object	Once was alive	Alive	Not alive	Because...
two plants in the school library		✓		... they grow, need water, air and food, make waste and can sense the world

This activity was a science enquiry because you were identifying
and classifying things.

Look at the diagrams below to see what each plant part does.

In sunlight each
leaf makes food

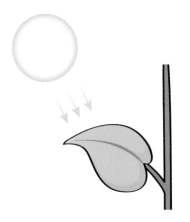

Seeds are made
by the flower

The stem holds up the plants
and water moves inside the stem

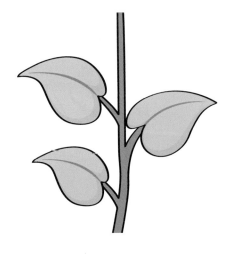

The roots hold the plant
down and get water from the soil

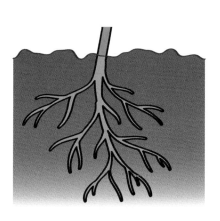

All parts of the plant need water.
Without water the plant will die.

The roots hold the plant down. They also absorb water
by taking it in from the soil. The water is then moved or
transported up the stem to all parts of the plant.

Activity 1

Looking at roots

You will need: a potted plant, soil, a larger pot, newspaper

If you are allergic to plant parts tell your teacher now.

Wash your hands if you have touched the plant or the soil.

Over newspaper, take a plant out of its pot. Take care not to damage the plant. Carefully observe the roots. Draw what you observe.

Does your plant need a new pot?
If it does, replant it in the bigger plant pot.

We can eat parts of some plants

Some plant parts are safe for people to eat. Some parts can be poisonous. The safe leaves, roots, stems and fruit are very good for you. We only ever eat safe plant parts. Which plant parts here are safe to eat?

Never eat parts of wild plants you find. Always check that plant parts are safe and clean before you eat them.

Question

1 Do you know a plant or plant part that is dangerous to eat?

Activity 2

Make a model plant

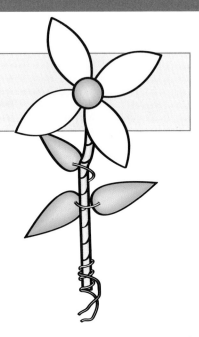

You will need: paper, card, a straw, string, glue, sticky tape

Making a model will help you learn about plants. You can touch the model and observe its parts.

Use the materials to make a model plant with a flower, stem, leaves and roots. Label your model.

Write a label to go beside your model. Your label should explain the way water enters and is transported inside the plant.

How am I doing?

Does your model look like a real plant?

Think like a scientist

Learning about leaves

You will need: books about plants, the internet, some leaves

Do not eat plants that you find.

Wash your hands after touching any plants.

Tell your teacher if you are allergic to any plants.

Marcus is asking some questions about leaves.

Why do some leaves fall each year?

Which is the biggest leaf?

Are all leaves green?
Is the top of a leaf the same as the bottom of a leaf?

Continued

Look at different leaves.

Talk to a friend. Think of some new questions about leaves. Look in books and on the internet for information that answers your questions.

Always take care on the internet. Use the school's safe systems.

Make a poster about leaves to show what you found out.

This was a science enquiry because you were researching.

How am I doing?

Pretend that a friend is a plant. Use a piece of paper to label their feet as roots and add more labels for the stem, leaves and flower. Say what each part does.

Does making a model help you learn about plants?

Look what I can do!

- ☐ I can say what the leaf, flower, stem and root do.
- ☐ I can make a model of a plant.
- ☐ I can make a drawing of plant roots.
- ☐ I can research leaves using books and the internet.
- ☐ I can stay safe while doing practical work.

> 1.3 Plants and light

We are going to:

- learn that plants need light and the right conditions to be healthy
- learn that baby plants grow from seeds
- talk about the importance of a fair test
- look for patterns in results
- make a conclusion from results
- make predictions and see if they are right.

Getting started

These young plants have started growing.

- Which plant is oldest?
- Which is youngest?
- What do these plants need to help them grow and be healthy?

conditions   germination
seedling   shoot   wilt

Plants need the right conditions

Plants need the right conditions to grow and be healthy.

The conditions they need are the right amount of:

- warmth
- water
- light
- air.

A healthy plant has strong roots, stems and leaves.

An unhealthy plant may have yellow leaves. The plant may wilt.

leaves are wilting and yellow

a healthy plant

an unhealthy plant

What do baby plants need?

The flowers of a plant make seeds. Inside each seed is a very small root shoot and a very small stem shoot, both ready to grow. The seed also has a store of food for the baby plant to start growing.

We call this germination.

The root shoot grows first to get water. Then the stem shoot grows.

The diagram shows what is inside a seed.

food store   stem shoot

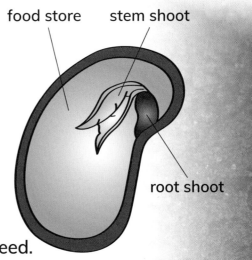

root shoot

The photograph shows how a seed starts growing. You can see a root shoot growing downwards and a stem shoot growing upwards.

Questions

1   The root shoot always grows downwards. Why is this?

2   The stem shoot always grows upwards. Why is this?

3   Look at what the children say.
    What do you think a plant needs to grow?

I think the seeds just need light to grow.

They just need soil.

I think they need water and light

4   Could a plant live without light?

Think like a scientist 1

Can plants grow well in the dark?

> **You will need:** six similar young plants in the same sized pots and same soil, a light place, a box

Place three plants in the light and three plants in the dark.

What do you predict will happen?

Make sure you wash your hands after touching plants or soil.

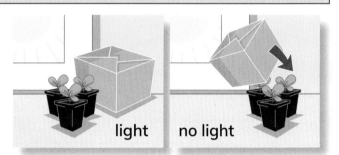

light   no light

Why do the plants need to be similar?

Why should the plants have the same soil and water?

Observe the plants every day for five days. Water them if the soil begins to dry. What differences do you notice? Record your observations on a table like this.

Day	Observations
1	On Day One we observed no differences between the plants in the light and the plants in the dark.
2	
3	
4	
5	

Was your prediction right?

You have been doing science.
How do you know this was a science enquiry?
What kind of science enquiry was this?

Why do seedling stems bend?

Baby plants are called seedlings.

Questions

5 These seedlings growing near a window are four days old. Why are the stems bent?

6 How could we change things so that the stems would grow upwards and straight?

Think like a scientist 2

How quickly will our plants grow?

You will need: plant seeds, soil, pots, ruler

Marcus and Zara grew a plant from a seed.
They measured it at 9 am each day for nine days.
Then they recorded their results on this graph.

How tall was the plant on day 1?

How many days did it take for the plant to grow to 4 cm?

On which days was the plant tallest?

How tall might it be on day 9?

What kind of science enquiry was this?

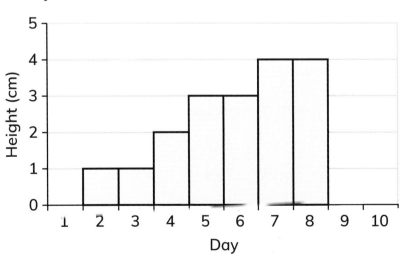

Think like a scientist 3

Light and plant growth

You will need: some seedlings, two plant trays, soil, seeds, a ruler, a place which is light, a place which is dark

Observe some seedlings. Look at their roots, stem and leaves.

Draw them.

Get two trays ready with soil. Sow ten seeds in each tray. Cover each seed with a little soil.

Give water to the seeds so that they do not dry out.

Place one tray in a light place and the other in a dark place.

Predict what you think will happen. Observe the trays over a number of days.

Record growth of the seeds in each tray. Use two charts like this one.

What do you observe about the way the seeds grow?

What is the difference between the seeds in the two trays?

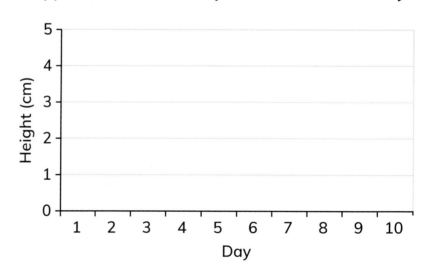

Was your prediction correct?

This was a science enquiry. Could we call this a fair test? Was it also another type of enquiry?

How am I doing?

Explain to a friend the importance of a fair test.

In this unit you are carrying out different types of science enquiry. How do the different types of enquiry help your learning of science?

Look what I can do!

☐ I know that plants need light and the right conditions to be healthy.

☐ I know that baby plants grow from seeds.

☐ I can talk about the importance of a fair test.

☐ I can look for patterns in results.

☐ I can make a conclusion from results.

☐ I can make predictions and see if they are right.

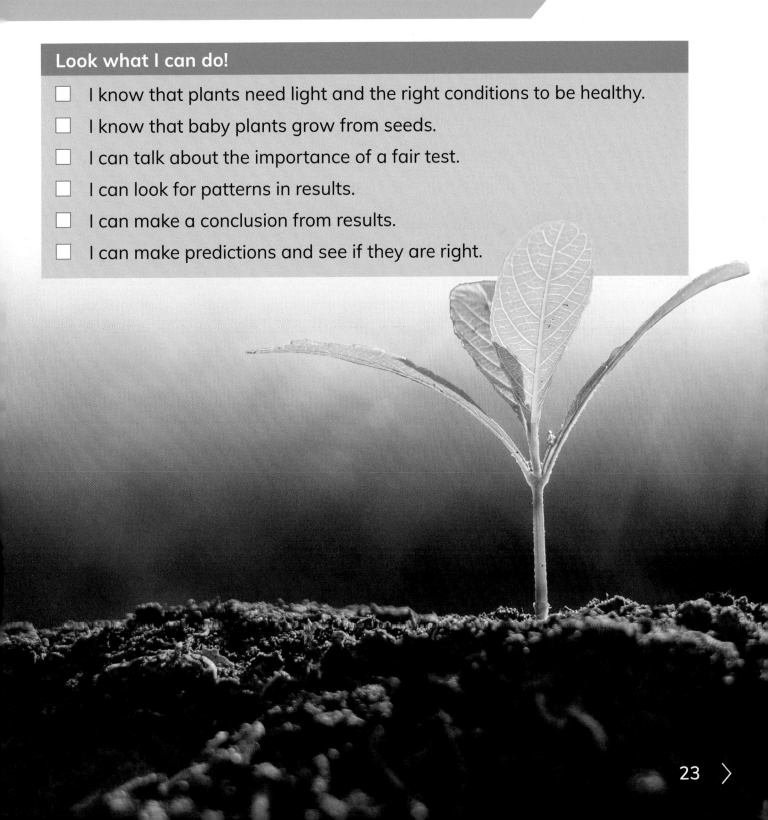

> 1.4 Plants need water and the right temperature

We are going to:

- investigate how plants need water to be healthy
- see how plants need the right temperature to be healthy
- see how water moves up through a plant stem
- measure using standard units
- make predictions and see if they are right
- make a conclusion from results
- read results from a bar chart and look for patterns in these results.

Getting started

- Why might the plants in both pictures not have enough water?

freezes   level   survive

All plants need water

Every part of a plant needs water. Water is absorbed by the roots from the soil. Look at the diagram to see how water moves around a plant.

Without enough water, plants will wilt and die.

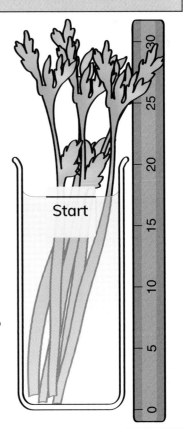

Leaves lose some water to the air around.

Leaves use water when they make food for the plant.

The stem transports water to the leaves and flowers.

The roots absorb water from the soil.

The roots transport water to the stem.

Think like a scientist 1

How much water do plant stems use?

You will need: a narrow jar, five leafy stems, water, a ruler, sticky labels

Place the stems into the jar.

Use a ruler to measure the height of the water. We call this the level of the water.

Predict what will happen to the water level after five days.

Mark the water level at the start. Measure and mark it at the same time each day.

Record how the water level changes.

Will you use mm, cm, m or just make a mark on the label? Which is best? Why?

What happened at the end of the test? Was your prediction right? Have you answered the question? How much water do plant stems use?

What kind of science enquiry was this?

Looking at a bar chart

Sofia did this investigation and recorded what happened in a bar chart.

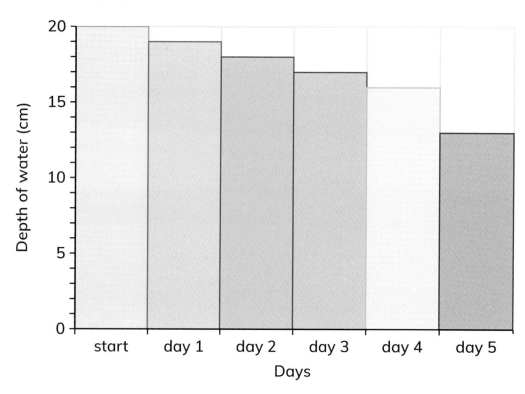

Questions

1   What happened to the level of the water on days 1 to 4?

2   What changed on day 5?

3   Why might this have happened?

4   What happened over the five days of the test?

Plants need the right temperature

Some plants can live in cold places and some in hot places. If it is very hot or very cold plants cannot survive. Too much heat or cold can kill them.

If it is too cold a plant's leaves cannot make food.
Water freezes, which means that it turns into
a solid and the plants cannot use it.

If it is too hot, the plant may have no water.
Roots, stems and leaves can dry and break.

Think like a scientist 2

Plants need the right temperature

You will need: 15 seeds, three plant pots, soil, a thermometer

Sow five seeds into each pot.
Cover the seeds in soil and give them water.

Place the pots in different places: one warm, one at room
temperature and one in the cold. Take the temperature in
each place. Keep them watered and don't let the soil
dry out.

Continued

Predict what will happen to the seeds in each pot.
Will they all start to grow at the same time?
Will they all grow well?

Observe them at the same time each day and record what happens to the seeds in each pot.

Will you draw them?

Will you measure them?

Will you record this on a table or graph?

What kind of science enquiry was this? Explain your answer.

Water can move up tall trees

Some trees are over 80 metres tall! Water has to travel all the way to the top. Water travels in lots of very narrow tubes in the main stem and goes to every leaf.

Think like a scientist 3

How does water move up a plant stem?

You will need: a cup of water, food colouring, a dropper or a teaspoon, a white flower, celery, a clock

Look at diagrams 1 and 2.

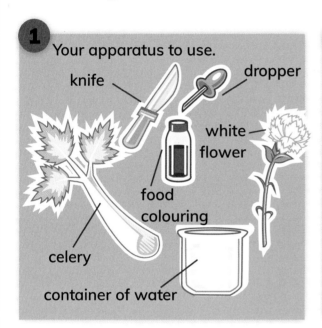

1 Your apparatus to use.
knife
dropper
white flower
food colouring
celery
container of water

2 Place the celery and the flower in the water. Add a few drops of colouring

Put the flower and celery in the pot of water.

Add a few drops food colouring to the water.

Predict what you think will happen.

Observe the pots every hour or two over a day.

Make drawings or take photographs to record what happens.

Was your prediction correct?

What does this tell you about water inside plants?

What kind of science enquiry was this?

Continued

How am I doing?

A friend asks you to look after a small potted plant for a week.
How much water would you need to give it? How do you know this?

In this topic you have used mathematics.
How does mathematics help you learn things in science?

Look what I can do!

☐ I can investigate how plants need water to be healthy.

☐ I know that plants need the right temperature to be healthy.

☐ I know how water moves up through a plant stem.

☐ I can measure using standard units.

☐ I can make predictions and see if they are right.

☐ I can make a conclusion from results.

☐ I can read results from a bar chart and look for patterns in these results.

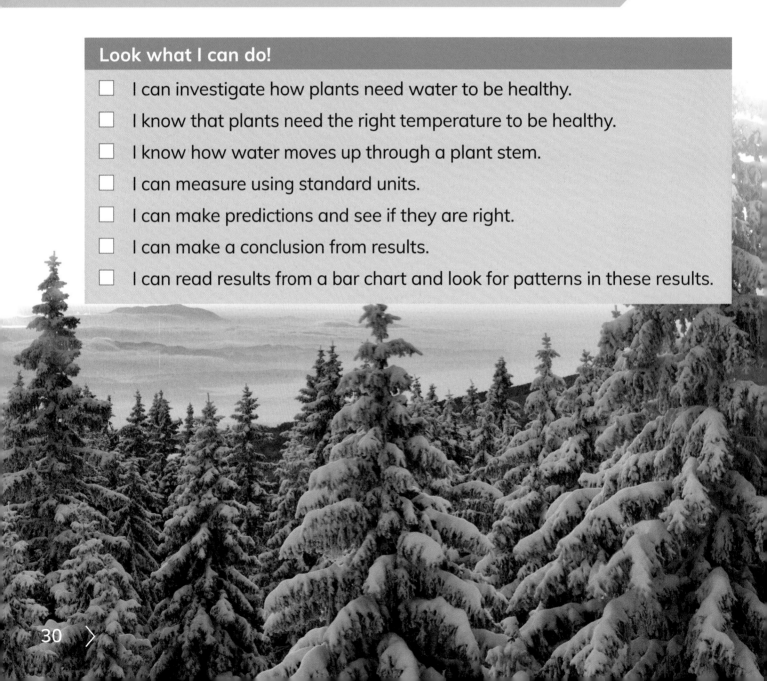

Project: How do plants use water?

Make a zig-zag book explaining the journey of water through a flowering plant.

A zig-zag book is like a 'fold up' poster. You need to draw and write to explain how water:

- is in the soil,
- is absorbed by the roots,
- moves up the stems,
- is used in leaves and flowers.

Start by researching in books and on the internet. Then write and draw diagrams to explain what happens to water in a plant.

Use arrows to show how the water moves in the plant.

Open the book to watch the poster grow!

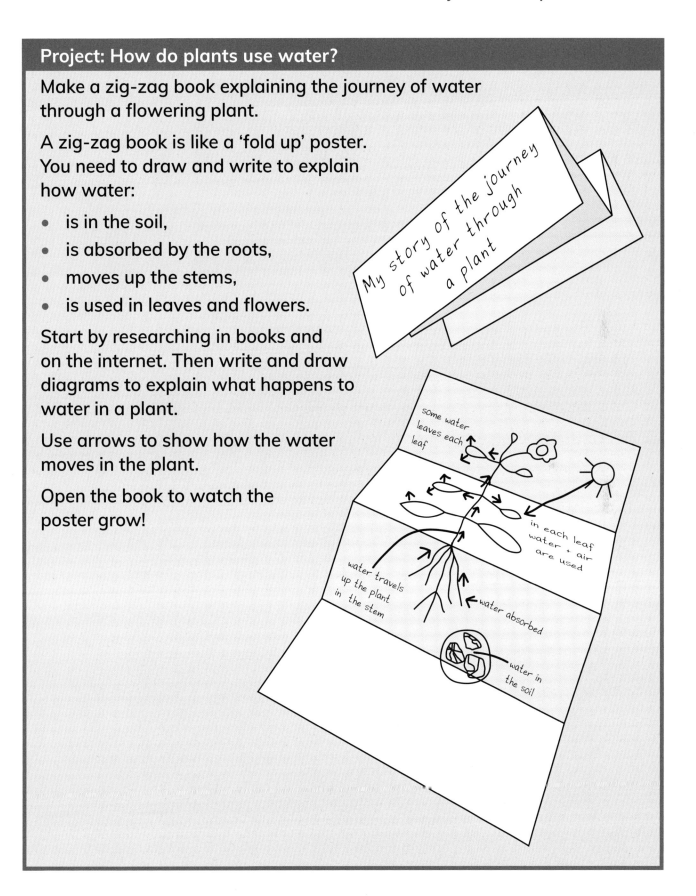

Check your progress

Talk about these questions.

1 Complete these sentences. You can use these words.

not alive   can have young   cannot have young   alive

I know this eagle is _____ because it _____

I know this candle is _____ because it _____

2 Here is a flowering plant.

Copy and complete these sentences.

A is the _____

B is the _____

C is the _____

D is the _____

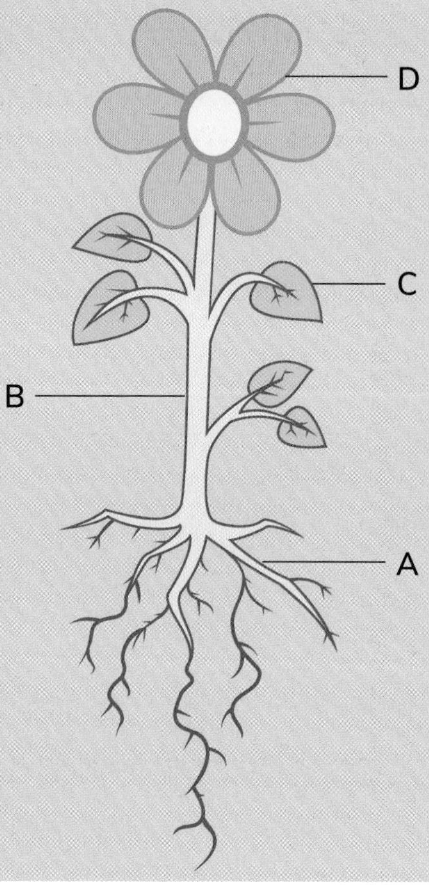

Continued

3 Copy and complete the sentences using the missing words.

You may use each word more than once.

roots	flowers	stem	leaves	water

Plants have _____ that are underground. These hold the

plant up and also absorb _____ . The water is transported to

the _____ and then up the plant to the _____ and

the _____ . The _____ make food for the plant.

The _____ are the place where seeds are made.

4 Which two of these does a plant need for it to grow?

Copy and complete this sentence.

A plant needs _____ and _____ to grow.

water	light
bread	plant pot

Continued

5 Luiz and Cheng are planning an investigation.

   a What are they investigating?

   b What should they keep the same to make the test fair?

   c Predict which plant will grow best.

Mixing materials

> 2.1 Solids, liquids and gases

We are going to:

- learn that materials can be solids, liquids or gases
- find out how the properties of solids and liquids are different
- observe materials and put them into groups
- find out which of the five types of science investigation we are doing
- identify risks and how to stay safe in practical work.

Getting started

Materials can be solids or liquids or gases.

This girl is blowing bubbles.

- Where is a gas in the picture?
- Where is a liquid in the picture?
- Where is a solid in the picture?

carbon dioxide
classifying
gas
liquid
nitrogen
solid

35 >

Solids, liquids and gases

All materials are either solids, liquids or gases.

Solids stay the same shape unless they are compressed, stretched, twisted or bent.

Liquids change shape easily and take the shape of the container they are in.

Gases spread out to fill the space around them.

A brick is a solid.

Water is a liquid.

The air inside the bubble is a gas.

Wood, metal and plastic are solids.

Water, milk and oil are liquids.

Air is a mixture of gases. It is mostly a gas called nitrogen but there is also some oxygen. We need oxygen to breathe. Nitrogen and oxygen have no colour so we can't see them. Some gases do have a colour, and some have a smell.

Hydrogen sulfide gas smells of rotten eggs.

Chlorine gas is yellow.

Think like a scientist 1

Making carbon dioxide gas

You will need: a cup, some bicarbonate of soda, some vinegar, a teaspoon and a candle

Sofia and Marcus are making a gas called carbon dioxide. They are going to pour the gas on the candle. Why do they need to be careful? How can they stay safe?

Now try making some carbon dioxide gas. How will you stay safe?

Put a little vinegar in the bottom of a cup. Next add half a teaspoon of bicarbonate of soda. Watch what happens.

You get lots of bubbles because the gas carbon dioxide is being made. This makes bubbles in the vinegar.

When the bubbles stop, the cup will be full of carbon dioxide gas. Carbon dioxide is clear and has no colour so you cannot see it. An adult will light your candle.

Carefully pour a little of the gas onto the flame of the candle. Do not pour any vinegar onto the candle. Watch what happens.

The flame goes out because it needs oxygen gas to burn, not carbon dioxide gas.

Think like a scientist 2

Sorting solids and liquids

You will need: a magnifying glass, some materials that are solid and some that are liquid

Observe the materials. Look closely, touch them and smell them.

Sort the solids into one group and the liquids into another. Another name for sorting is classifying.

How am I doing?

Have a look at how others have sorted their materials. Tell them whether you think they have put the materials into the right groups.

Think of some materials that would go into a 'gas' group.

There are five types of scientific enquiry:
- researching
- fair testing
- identifying and classifying
- looking for patterns
- observing things for a long time.

Which type of scientific enquiry is the sorting activity?

Look what I can do!

☐ I can name two examples of materials that are usually solid, two that are liquid and two that are gases.

☐ I can describe the different properties of solids and liquids.

☐ I can sort materials into solid, liquid and gas groups by making observations.

☐ I can identify which of the five types of science investigation I am doing.

☐ I can explain how I stayed safe in practical work.

> 2.2 Separating mixtures

We are going to:

- **learn about mixtures and how to separate them**
- **observe the properties of materials in mixtures**
- **choose equipment to separate mixtures**
- **draw clear diagrams.**

Getting started

These beans are all mixed together.

- Tell a friend how you would separate the beans into the different types. What could you use to help?

- Draw diagrams to show your ideas.

equipment
magnet
magnetic
mixture
non-magnetic
separate
sieve

Using equipment

When two or more materials are mixed together it is called a mixture.

Some mixtures can be separated by hand, but this is very slow. The equipment this man is holding is used to separate soil from old plant roots. It has many small holes for the soil to fall through. The roots are too big to go through the holes. This piece of equipment is called a sieve. Using the right equipment makes separating mixtures much faster.

This magnet is separating a mixture of different metals. When materials are made into a mixture the properties of each material do not change. Some of the metal in this mixture is magnetic and some is non-magnetic.

Questions

1 What is a mixture?

2 What word can we use for things like sieves, magnets and other objects that help us to do things?

3 How does a sieve work?

This girl is separating different types of plastic by hand. In some countries, children do this to make enough money to buy food.

Think like a scientist 1

Using a sieve

You will need: a mixture of salt and beans, a sieve and a plate

Marcus has mixed up the beans and the salt. How can he separate this mixture?

Use a sieve and a plate to separate a mixture of beans and salt.

Draw and label a diagram that shows the mixture and how you used the sieve.

Think like a scientist 2

An amazing mixture

You will need: a mixture of sand, rice and paper clips and some equipment to choose from

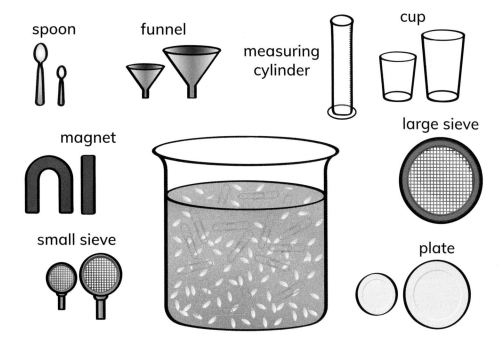

Think about how you will separate a mixture of sand, rice and paper clips.

What equipment will you need? How will you use it?

Draw and label some diagrams to show how you separated the mixture.

How am I doing?

Look at a friend's diagrams.

Have they labelled the equipment? Are their diagrams neat?

Tell them if there is something they could add or change to make their diagram better.

Did you find it easy or difficult to choose the equipment you needed? Say why you found it easy or difficult.

If you chose something you did not use, next time think carefully about what you are going to do before you choose your equipment.

Look what I can do!

- ☐ I can describe some different mixtures and how to separate them.
- ☐ I can talk about the properties of different materials in a mixture.
- ☐ I can choose the right equipment to separate a mixture.
- ☐ I can draw clear diagrams.

› 2.3 Dissolving

We are going to:

- find out that, in a mixture of a solid and a liquid, sometimes the solid dissolves

- ask a scientific question, then plan a scientific enquiry to find the answer

- record observations in tables and diagrams

- learn how we can stay safe in an investigation.

dissolve
insoluble
soluble
transparent

Getting started

I put some sugar in but now it has gone.

You can still taste the sugar.

I think the sugar is still there, but you can't find it with spoon.

SUGAR

Sofia, Marcus and Arun are not sure what has happened to the sugar.

- Write down who you think is right.

Some solids dissolve when they are mixed with a liquid. This means the solid breaks into pieces that are too small to see. When the solid has dissolved we cannot see it but it is still there.

Many liquids are see through. We say they are transparent. When a solid dissolves in a transparent liquid the liquid stays transparent but might change colour.

We describe solids that dissolve in a liquid as soluble. Sugar dissolves in water, so sugar is soluble in water. We describe solids that do not dissolve in a liquid as insoluble.

Sand does not dissolve in water, so sand is insoluble in water.

An insoluble solid in a liquid is a mixture and can be easily separated.

A soluble solid in a liquid is still a mixture but is more difficult to separate.

Questions

1 What word describes a solid that will dissolve in a liquid?

2 What word describes a solid that will not dissolve in a liquid?

3 Sugar dissolves in water. Name any other solids that dissolve in water.

Activity

Dissolving sweets

> **You will need:** some coloured sweets, a plate and some water

Some sweets are made of coloured sugar.

Put some of these sweets into a little water to see what happens when the sugar dissolves.

Draw a diagram to show what happens.

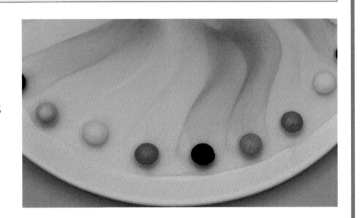

Think like a scientist 1

How much salt will dissolve in water?

> **You will need:** three drinking glasses, a spoon, some salt and some water

Look at the picture to see how to set up the investigation.

Put half a spoon of salt into each glass of water. Stir each one.

Observe to see if the salt dissolves.

Then add another half spoon of salt to each glass, stir and observe again.

Continued

Keep doing this until the salt stops dissolving.

Talk about your predictions before you start.

Write your results in a table like this.

Amount of water	How many teaspoons of salt dissolved

Questions

1 In which glass of water did the least salt dissolve?

2 In which glass of water did the most salt dissolve?

3 How does the amount of water affect the amount of salt that will dissolve?

Think like a scientist 2

Asking questions about dissolving

You will need: a spoon, some cups and some water, vinegar and cooking oil or other liquids and some salt, sugar, sand, flour, jelly crystals or other solids

Arun has a scientific question.

Question 1.
Which of the five types of scientific enquiry will Arun need to use to find the answer: research, fair testing, observing over time, identifying and classifying or pattern seeking?

In your group, look at the materials and ask your own scientific question like this.

Which liquids will _____ dissolve in?

Plan your own fair test by drawing a diagram to show what you are going to do.

Which liquids will salt dissolve in?

In a fair test you change one thing, measure or observe one thing and keep the rest the same. In this test the thing you change is the liquid. The thing you observe is whether the solid will dissolve.

Question 2.
To make the test fair, what will you need to keep the same?

Label your diagram to show the things you will keep the same.

Continued

Do not taste any of the materials you use in this investigation.

Question 3.
Why is it unsafe to taste the materials?

Now do your fair test and write sentences to record your results.

Use the words *soluble* and *insoluble* in your sentences, like this.

Salt is soluble in water and vinegar.

Salt is insoluble in cooking oil.

How am I doing?

Have a look at another group's diagram.
Have they made it a fair test?

Tell them if there is anything else they need to keep the same.

It can be hard to see whether a solid has all dissolved.
Did you do anything to make it easier to see?
Is there anything that would have made it even easier?

Look what I can do!

☐ I can name two materials that dissolve in water and one that does not.

☐ I can ask a scientific question and plan the right type of scientific enquiry to find the answer.

☐ I can record my observations in tables and diagrams.

☐ I can explain how to stay safe in an investigation.

> 2.4 Filtering

We are going to:

- find out how to separate a mixture of a solid and a liquid
- draw clear diagrams
- record observations in tables and diagrams
- use our results to say whether our predictions were correct or not
- do practical work safely.

Getting started

If this dirty water was all you had to drink, what would you do?

- How could you separate the dirt from the water?
- Talk to a friend about your ideas.

filter
filter paper
funnel
layer

How does a filter work?

Dirty water is a mixture of solid and liquid materials. We can separate the insoluble solids from the liquid by pouring the mixture through a filter. A filter has holes that let some of the mixture pass through. Solids in the mixture stay in the filter because the pieces are too big to pass through the holes. A sieve is a kind of filter but most filters have much smaller holes.

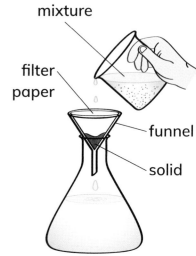

mixture

filter paper

funnel

solid

Scientists use filter paper to separate mixtures. Filter paper has very tiny holes and stays strong when it gets wet so it does not tear easily. A funnel is a cone-shaped piece of equipment that can be used to support the filter paper.

Question

1   Use the picture to explain to a friend how this filter could be used to separate a mixture of sand and water.

Think like a scientist 1

Make a simple filter

You will need: two cups, a paper towel, some sand and some water

Arun and Sofia are using things they find in their classroom to make a filter. They have a plastic cup and a paper towel. They want to use their simple filter to separate a mixture of sand and water.

Make a simple filter like this. What do you predict will happen when you try to separate the sand and water?

Try it to see whether your prediction is correct.

What other mixtures could you separate using a simple filter like this? Talk with your friends about your ideas.

Filtering waste water

Large filters like these are used to make waste water clean.

The water drips through different layers including rock, gravel and sand. The different layers filter out different-sized pieces of waste.

Think like a scientist 2

Make a layered filter

You will need: some dirty water in a cup, some sand, some gravel, some stones, some cotton wool or fabric and a large plastic bottle that has been cut in half

This is a layered filter. There are layers of different materials in the bottle. Each layer covers the material below.

Observe the dirty water carefully. What solid pieces can you see? How large are they? What size holes will you need to stop the solids going through the filter?

Be careful with any sharp edges where the plastic has been cut. Do not drink the water.

— small stones
— sand layer
— cotton wool layer

Make a filter with different layers that you think will make the water clean.

Continued

- Draw and label a diagram of your layered filter.
- Record a prediction about how clean you think the water will be when it comes out.
- Use your filter to filter the water.
- Draw and label a diagram of the water that comes out.
- Record whether your prediction was correct.
- How could you make a better filter? Would your filter work better with a different fabric, more sand or more gravel?
- Predict what would make your filter better.
- Now change your filter and use it again to see whether your new prediction is correct.
- Draw more diagrams to show your new filter and the water that comes out.

How am I doing?

Talk with another group about how you changed your filters. Did the changes make the filters better?

Listen to what they think will make your filter even better. Do you agree or disagree?

Look what I can do!

- ☐ I can draw diagrams to show how to separate a mixture of a solid and a liquid.
- ☐ I can draw clear diagrams.
- ☐ I can record my observations in tables and diagrams.
- ☐ I can use my results to say whether my predictions were correct or not.
- ☐ I can do practical work safely.

> 2.5 Separating materials from rocks

We are going to:

- **find out where materials come from**
- **ask scientific questions and work out which type of scientific enquiry can be used to find the answers**
- **research answers to questions using books, videos or the internet.**

Getting started

Where do materials come from?

This flow chart shows where paper comes from.

paper > wood > trees > found in the ground

- Draw some flow charts like this to show where other materials come from.
- Have a look at flow charts drawn by other learners in your class. Do you agree with them?

aluminium   carbon   diesel   flow chart   fuels   global warming
iron   natural gas   oil   ore   petrol   smelting

Materials from the Earth

Planet Earth is the source of all the materials that we use.

All materials that have to be made, like plastic and metal, are made from materials that are natural.

Most plastic is made from oil which is found in the ground.

Metals are made from rocks in the ground called ores.

Metals and ores

This is an ore called bauxite.

It is used to make a metal called aluminium.

This is an ore called hematite.

It is used to make a metal called iron.

The metal has to be separated from other material in the ore to make pure metal. The metal ore is heated and melted to separate the metal. This is called smelting.

Think like a scientist 1

Asking questions about metals

You will need: access to the internet, books and videos about metals

There are many different metals.

How many of these have you heard of?

 steel silver zinc gold lead chrome copper

There are many questions you could ask about metals.

What ore is zinc made from?

What is copper used for?

Where is gold found?

Choose one metal and write questions about it.

Use a book, a video or the internet to find out the answers and record them.

Which of the five types of scientific enquiry will you use to find the answers: research, fair testing, observing over time, identifying and classifying or pattern seeking?

Make a poster about your metal to show what you find out.

Oil and natural gas

Natural gas is a gas found underground. We burn it to cook, heat our homes and to make electricity. Oil is a liquid found underground. The oil is heated to make useful liquids and gases. The petrol and diesel we burn in cars and lorries are made from oil.

Materials that we burn are called fuels. Fuels like natural gas, crude oil, petrol and diesel all contain a material called carbon. When we burn these materials carbon dioxide gas is made. Too much carbon dioxide in the air is making the Earth get warmer. This is called global warming.

This oil rig has drilled a hole into the rocks under the sea and is pumping out oil.

Think like a scientist 2

Researching plastic

You will need: access to the internet, books and videos about plastic

Most plastic is strong and flexible. This means that plastic can last a very long time. Most types of plastic are made from oil, but plastic can be made from any material that contains lots of carbon. Many materials that come from plants and animals can be used to make a type of plastic called bioplastic.

Continued

Ask a question about plastic.

Use a book, a video or the internet to research the answer. Record your questions and answers, then talk about what you find out with your class.

What is ... ?   How might ... ?

Where can ... ?

Who invented ... ?

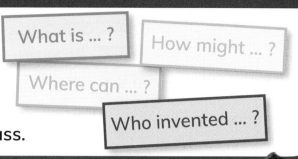

Questions

1   What is an ore?

2   Name three materials that are made from oil.

3   Why can burning fuels cause a problem?

In this topic you used books, videos or the internet to do some research.

Which of these do you think is easiest to learn from and why?

Look what I can do!

☐   I can name the source of all the materials we use.

☐   I can say where oil, natural gas, metal and some other materials are found.

☐   I can ask a scientific question and say which type of scientific enquiry can be used to find the answer.

☐   I can research answers to questions using books, videos or the internet.

Project: Designing a reusable object

We make many things from plastic that we only use once. Most plastic lasts a really long time. All these plastic objects ended up as rubbish on a beach.

We call things we only use once disposable. We should make disposable objects from materials that do not last a long time.

Things we use many times are called reusable. We should use reusable objects instead of disposable objects whenever we can.

These disposable objects are made from wood or paper.

The blue bags are made from plastic. This reusable shopping bag is made from natural fabric.

Look at the picture of plastic objects on the beach.

Are there any disposable things that could be made of a better material?

Continued

Could a reusable object be used instead?

Design a reusable object or a disposable object made of a better material.
Make a poster showing your new object.
Write about why it is better than the disposable object made of plastic.

Reusable aluminium bottle.
Saves 100s of plastic bottles.
Can be used forever!

Check your progress

Talk about the answers to these questions.

1 Which of these materials are solids? Which are liquids? Which are gases? How do you know?

water   cooking oil   sugar   carbon dioxide   natural gas

petrol   sand   aluminium   plastic

2 Which equipment would you use to separate these mixtures?

beans and salt

paper clips and salt

sand and water

Continued

3   Marcus, Sofia and Arun are talking about how to separate a mixture of sugar and water.

Do you agree or disagree with their ideas?

The sugar has dissolved so it will go through the filter.

The water will go through, but the sugar will stay in the filter.

Only some of the sugar will go through the filter.

4   Which of these flow charts are correct?

A   iron > hematite > found in the ground

B   plastic > oil > found in the ground

C   petrol > wood > trees > grown in the ground

> 3.1 Shadows

We are going to:

- investigate how light can pass through transparent materials and is blocked by opaque materials

- sort materials into transparent or opaque materials

- learn that shadows are formed when light from a source is blocked by an object

- collect and record observations in tables then interpret the results.

- make a prediction and see if it is right.

> blocked
> opaque
> shadow

Getting started

- Look at the picture. What might be the light source?

- Which child is riding a bicycle?
  Draw the shadow of the child riding the scooter.

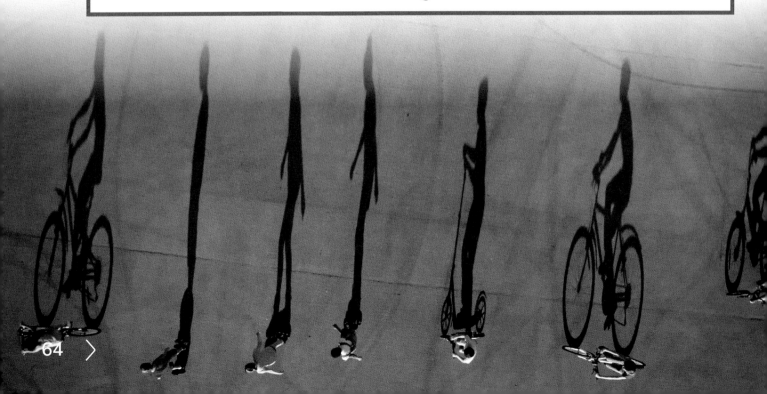

How are shadows made?

A shadow is made when light is blocked by an opaque object.

Light cannot pass through an opaque material. This means that a dark area is made. This is a shadow.

Shadows have no colour. They are always dark.

Shadows have no details like eyes or a mouth.

The shadow may not be the same shape and size as the object.

Questions

1 Does everything have a shadow?

2 Mia has two shadows. Why is this?

3 If Mia moves, how might the shadows change?

Activity 1

Making shadows in the sunlight

> **You will need:** a sunny place, chalk

Emeka is using his opaque body to make shadow shapes in the sunlight.

Umar draws around the shadows with chalk.

Try this outside.
Check to see if the shadow is the same shape as the person.

Activity 2

Making shadow puppets

You will need: card, scissors, a stick, sticky tape, a light source, a wall

Never look into the light from a bright light source. It can damage your eyes.

Sara and Nasreen are making shadow puppets. They use card which is opaque.

Try making your own shadow puppets. Tell other people how the shadow is made. Use the words opaque, light source and blocks.

Transparent materials

Some materials are not opaque. They let light through. They are transparent. Transparent materials do not make a shadow. We can see things clearly through transparent materials.

Questions

4   Glass is very good for making windows. Why is this?

5   Why do shops use so much glass in their front windows?

Be careful with glass. If it breaks it can cut you.

Think like a scientist

Opaque or transparent?

You will need: some different materials, a flashlight

Your teacher will give you some materials.
Do you think they are opaque or transparent?

Record your predictions in a table.

Test each material with a flashlight. Does light pass through?

Now record your results.

Material	Is the material opaque?	
	My prediction	Result of the test
glass	transparent	transparent

Were your predictions correct?

Which materials would not make good windows?

Why would they not make good windows?

How am I doing?

If you wanted to make a sunshade, would you use an opaque or transparent material?
Which materials might make a good sunshade?

Does it help your learning to use the right science words? Can using words like opaque and transparent outside the classroom help you to learn even more about science?

Look what I can do!

☐ I can investigate how light can pass through transparent materials and is blocked by opaque materials.

☐ I can sort materials into transparent and opaque materials.

☐ I know that shadows are formed when light from a source is blocked by an object.

☐ I can collect and record observations in tables then interpret the results.

☐ I can make a prediction and see if I was right.

> 3.2 Changing shadows

We are going to:

- investigate how shadows can change
- explore how shadows are formed when light is blocked by an object
- make a prediction and see if it is right
- record results in a table then interpret these results
- describe simple patterns in results and make a conclusion from results.

Getting started

- Why are these shadows so long?
- How might these shadows get longer or shorter?

conclusion

Looking at shadows

Do you ever see shadows in your classroom?

If there is a bright light source you may be able to see shadows made by objects. Do you ever see the shadows move or change size or shape?

A shadow can look like the object making the shadow.

Sometimes the shadow of an object looks very different to the object.

Question

1   Identify these things from the shadows:

a car   a cyclist

a plane   a fish

Activity 1

Shadow shapes

You will need:
a flashlight, a small toy, classroom lights turned off or down, a table top

Sofia is investigating shadows.
She moves the toy and observes as its shadow changes.

Hold your flashlight pointing down at the toy.
Draw the toy and its shadow.

Continued

Now move the toy. Observe how the shadow changes.
Draw the new shadow shape.

Why did the shadow change shape?

How many different shadow shapes could you make?

Why were the lights turned off for this investigation?

Activity 2

Making animal shapes

You will need: a bright light source, a screen, a darkened room

**Do not look directly at a bright light source.
It may damage your eyes.**

Try making these shadow animals with your hands.
Notice how the shadow shapes change when you
move your hands.

How can you make a shadow grow and then get smaller?

Think like a scientist

How can shadows grow?

You will need: a flashlight, card, a wooden stick, two rulers, a table top, paper, card, scissors, sticky tape

You are going to investigate how the shadow of an object changes as you move the object closer to the source of light.

Use the card to make a start that is 2cm across. Look at the picture to see how to measure the star.

Stick the star onto the end of a wooden stick.

Hold a flashlight 30 cm from a table top pointing down onto the paper.

Now hold the star in the light at a height of 2 cm from the table top. Draw around the shadow on the paper. Measure the width of the shadow.

Continued

Predict what will happen to the width of the shadow as you move the star towards the light source.

Describe the pattern in your results.

Make a **conclusion** from your results. Finish this sentence.

	Size of shadows cast by a star which is 2 cm across		
Height of object (star) above table	Predicted width of shadow	Width of shadow
2 cm	2 cm	2 cm
4 cm	4 cm	
6 cm	6 cm	

As an object moves towards a light source its shadow gets _____ .

How am I doing?

Draw a picture of a flashlight shining on a wall.
Draw your hand in the light and the shadow it casts on the wall.
Explain to a friend how you can make the shadow smaller and bigger when you keep the flashlight still.

Does measuring things help you understand them?

Look what I can do!

☐ I can investigate how shadows can change.

☐ I can make a prediction and see if it is right.

☐ I can record results in a table then interpret the results.

☐ I can describe simple patterns in results.

☐ I can make a conclusion from results.

> 3.3 Transparent materials

We are going to:

- investigate how light can pass through transparent materials and is blocked by opaque materials

- identify risks and explain how to stay safe during practical work

- make a prediction and see if it is correct

- describe simple patterns in results

- record results using a table and make a conclusion.

Getting started

Clean water is a transparent material.

We can see things clearly through it.

- Some water is opaque and some is transparent. How might transparent water become opaque?

goggles
visor

Where do we use transparent materials?

We use many transparent materials in homes, buildings and cars. Transparent materials allow us to see things.

Glass is a transparent material. Some glass is very strong. People are walking on glass on this bridge.

Transparent materials allow light to pass through them. We can see things clearly through them. Often transparent things protect our eyes or protect us from the weather.

Glasses and goggles help us to see clearly. They are made from transparent materials.

Question

1 Why are dark sunglasses no help when we are indoors?

Activity 1

Transparent materials used around school

You will need: paper, a pencil, a digital camera if possible

Always take care with glass. It can break and be very dangerous.

Have a look around your classroom and parts of your school.
Where do you see transparent materials?
Why is that material needed for this job? What is the material?
Draw pictures to show how the materials are used.
You might take photographs of different materials.

How am I doing?

If you were buying curtains to make the classroom dark,
how would you describe the curtain material you wanted
to buy to the shopkeeper?

Activity 2

Make a pair of sunglasses

You will need: transparent coloured plastic, card, scissors, sticky tape

Never look at the Sun, even with sunglasses it can hurt your eyes.

Make a pair of sunglasses.

Draw and cut out a pair of glasses frames. Stick onto them a transparent material.

Try your glasses. Can you see everything? How do things look different?

Very dark goggles

In some places the Sun is very bright. It would hurt your eyes badly. This snowboarder needs very dark goggles. The goggles need to be a little opaque.

Questions

2 Why do the goggles need to be a little opaque?

3 Why should the goggles not be too opaque?

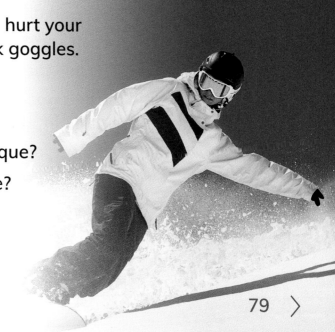

Think like a scientist

Can we make sunglasses darker?

You will need: transparent coloured plastic, scissors, a flashlight

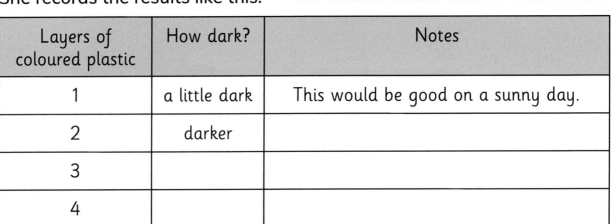

You can use more layers of coloured plastic to make even darker sunglasses.

Zara is testing the layers of coloured plastic to see how dark sunglasses could be.

She records the results like this.

Layers of coloured plastic	How dark?	Notes
1	a little dark	This would be good on a sunny day.
2	darker	
3		
4		

Predict which will be the darkest set of layers.

Now carry out tests on different numbers of layers of coloured plastic.

Was your prediction correct?

Record your results. Is there a pattern in the results?

Which would make a good pair of sunglasses for a very bright day? If you wore these at night, would you be able to see?

Why should you never look at the Sun, even when you are wearing sunglasses?

Complete this conclusion.

Every layer we add makes the sunglasses _____ .

Visors for astronauts

Astronauts work in space where the Sun is very bright. They need a transparent material for their visors so that they can see. But the visor needs also to stop the sunlight hurting the astronaut's eyes. This astronaut's visor is so dark we cannot see her face. We can only see the reflection of her hands.

Questions

4   Why don't astronauts wear sunglasses inside their helmet?

5   If you wore an astronaut's visor in class, how would the room look?

Do you find some parts of science easier to learn about than others? Does it help if you can do a science investigation?

Look what I can do!

☐ I can investigate how light can pass through transparent materials and is blocked by opaque materials.

☐ I can identify risks and say how to stay safe.

☐ I can make a prediction and see if it is correct.

☐ I can describe simple patterns in results.

☐ I can record my results using a table and make a conclusion.

> 3.4 Translucent materials

We are going to:

- talk about transparent, translucent and opaque materials

- stay safe when using glass in an investigation

- record observations in tables then interpret the results

- make predictions and see if they are right

- draw a diagram to show how translucent material scatters light.

Getting started

- These children are telling a story. How are the shadows made?
  How do we see them on the large sheet of fabric?

frosted
scatter
translucent

Translucent glass

Glass is usually transparent. It lets the light through.

You can read through transparent glass.

The arrows on these diagrams show how the light travels.

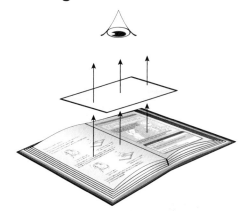

Transparent glass: light
passes straight through

Light from objects passes straight
through: we see things clearly

Sometimes glass is frosted or patterned to make it translucent.
The light is scattered by translucent glass so it is harder to see
through it. It is hard to read through translucent materials.

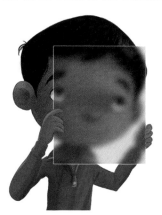

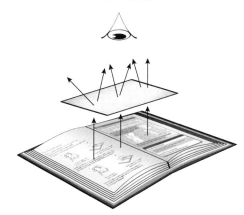

Translucent glass:
light is scattered

Light from objects is scattered:
things do not look clear

Translucent glass is useful when we don't want people to
see clearly through the glass. We can also make shadows
on translucent materials.

Activity 1

Make a shadow theatre screen

You will need: a large box with one side removed, greaseproof paper, sticky tape, lollipop sticks, card, scissors, a darkened room, a flashlight

Zara has made a theatre screen with translucent paper. She uses opaque card to make shadow puppets that tell a story on the screen. Zara shines a flashlight to make the shadows.

Make your own theatre screen using a box and translucent paper. Use opaque card to make shadow puppet shapes.

Think like a scientist

Transparent or translucent?

You will need: a sheet of clear plastic, other transparent and translucent things, a page of writing

Be careful if you are using glass.
Glass can smash and the sharp bits may cut you.

Continued

Sofia is testing different materials to see if they are transparent or translucent.

You can test a material to see if it is transparent.

Hold the writing on one side of the clear plastic. Can you look through the clear plastic and read the writing?

I can read words through the clear plastic, it is transparent.

I can't read through the translucent materials because they scatter the light.

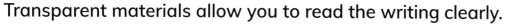

Transparent materials allow you to read the writing clearly.

Translucent materials do not allow you to read the writing clearly.

Look through the other materials and see if you can read the writing. Write your results in a table.

	Prediction	Test
Drinking glass	transparent	transparent

Were your predictions correct?

Activity 2

Opaque, translucent or transparent?

You will need: a collection of opaque, translucent and transparent materials, a long string, paper clips, a flashlight, scissors, three labels: opaque, translucent, transparent

Arrange materials in order from opaque to transparent.

Test the materials with a flashlight. Check if they block light (opaque), scatter light (translucent) or let through the light (transparent).

Continued

How am I doing?

A friend says 'Translucent materials are a source of light'.
How would you explain what translucent materials really are?
Draw a diagram to help.

Look what I can do!

- ☐ I can talk about transparent, translucent and opaque materials.
- ☐ I can stay safe when using a glass sheet.
- ☐ I can record observations in tables then interpret the results.
- ☐ I can make predictions and see if they are correct.
- ☐ I can draw a diagram to show how translucent materials scatter light.

Project: Opaque, translucent and transparent materials in a house

You will need: card, transparent plastic, translucent paper, sticky tape, scissors, glue, marker pens

When builders make a house, they need lots of materials. The builder needs to use their science skills and knowledge to choose the right materials with the right properties for each part of the house. For example, some materials will need to be waterproof, some transparent, and others will need to be very strong.

Draw the front of a new home with a window in the front door, a window to the kitchen and a window for the bathroom. Add to your drawing using some of the materials you have been given.

List which materials will be opaque, transparent and translucent.

Add some other things to the drawing which are made from opaque, transparent or translucent materials.

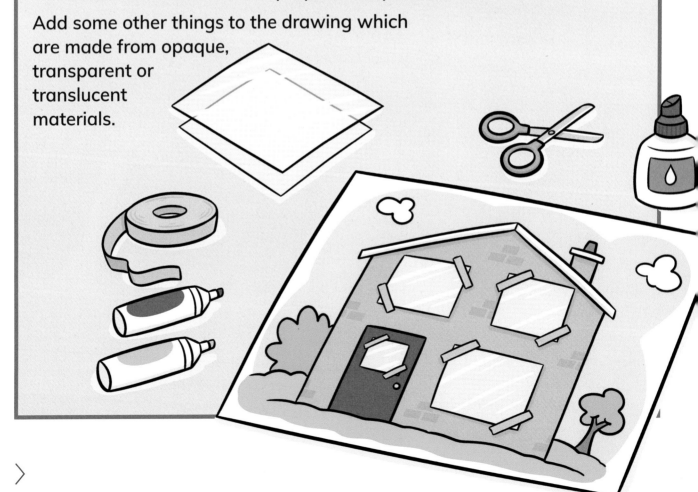

Check your progress

Talk about these questions.

1 How can this boy make a shadow with his puppet?

2 What is wrong with these shadows?

Continued

3 Which of these materials is opaque or transparent?

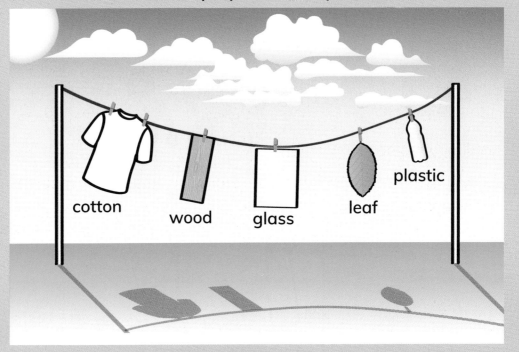

4 Which glass is transparent and which is translucent?

Staying alive

> 4.1 Human organs

We are going to:

- find out where the important organs are in the human body

- find out what body organs do

- look at results recorded on a bar chart and look for patterns in these results

- make a conclusion from results

- make predictions and see if they are right

- collect observations in a table.

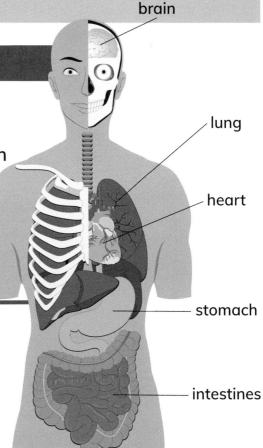

brain

lung

heart

stomach

intestines

Getting started

Look at this picture of the inside of the human body.

Point to your own body to show the position of your brain, heart, lungs, stomach and intestines.

- Write a sticky note to say what you think each of these parts of the body does.

beat	blood	blood vessels
brain	breath	breathe
exercise	heart rate	intestines
lungs	muscle	nutrients
organ	pulse	stomach

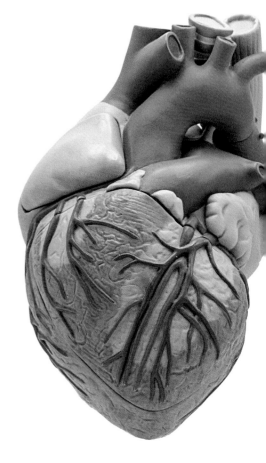

Your heart

Your body has many parts. Some of these parts are called organs. Each organ does an important job in making your body work.

Your heart is an organ. It pushes blood around your body. Your heart is made of muscle which is strong and can squeeze blood into the tubes called blood vessels. Each squeeze of the heart is called a beat. Each beat of the heart pushes blood into and around your blood vessels. If you exercise you may feel your heart beating faster.

Using a model of the heart helps you learn about the heart.

To help you grow, you need to look after your heart with a healthy diet and by taking exercise each day.

By feeling your pulse in your wrist, you can count your heartbeats. You will feel your pulse as your heart beats. The speed of beating is your heart rate.

Questions

1 Can you feel your heart beating?

2 Have you felt your heart beat faster after you have been running or playing?

Think like a scientist 1

Exercise and heart rate

You will need: a stopwatch

Marcus and Zara are investigating how their hearts speed up when they exercise.

Your heart rate went up from 65 beats per minute to 85 beats per minute.

Zara
at rest -
65 beats in a minute.
after exercise
85 beats in a minute.

Continued

Look at the bar chart.

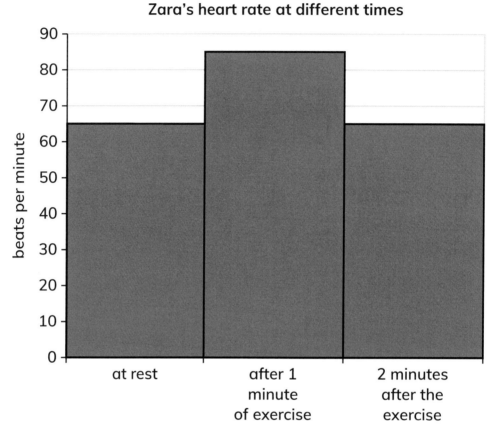

Zara's heart rate at different times

beats per minute

at rest | after 1 minute of exercise | 2 minutes after the exercise

Time we measured heart rate

Answer these questions.

1 What was Zara's heart rate before the exercise?

2 What was Zara's heart rate after exercise?

3 What was Zara's heart rate after two minutes of rest?

4 The bar chart shows a pattern. Do you think the same pattern always happens when you exercise and then stop?

Now use a watch to take the pulse of a friend at rest, after 1 minute's exercise and again two minutes later. Do you see a similar pattern of an increase in heart rate followed by a return to the resting heart rate?

Your lungs

In your chest are your two lungs. When you breathe in your chest gets bigger and sucks air into your lungs. Oxygen in the air then moves into your blood.

If you exercise your body will need more oxygen. Your lungs will take more breaths each minute so that there is more oxygen in your blood. Children take more breaths than an adult because their lungs are smaller.

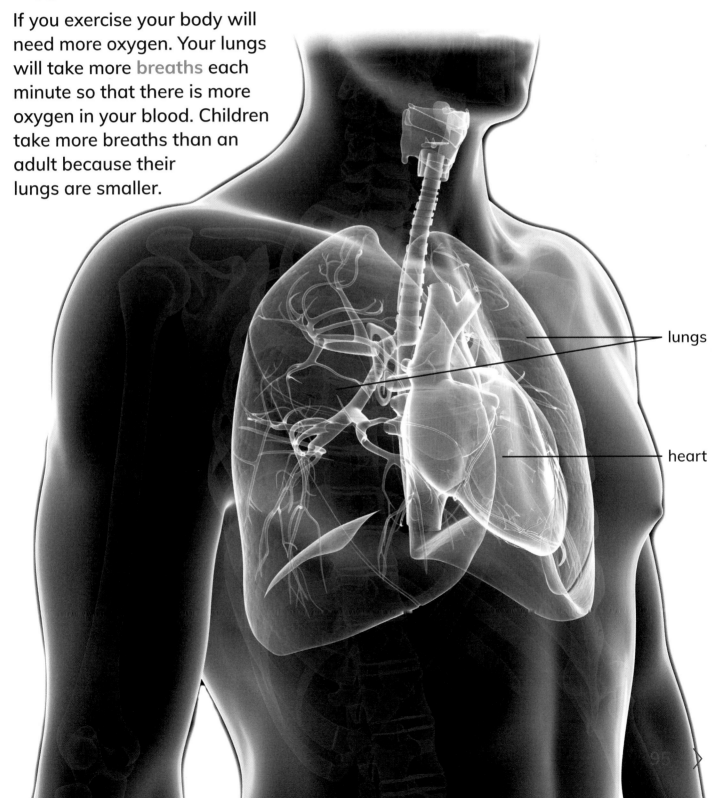

lungs

heart

Think like a scientist 2

How many breaths in one minute?

You will need: a stopwatch

Predict how many breaths you will take in one minute. Predict the number at rest and then predict the number after exercise.

While you sit at rest, count the times you breathe in during one minute.

This is your breathing rate, at rest.

Then after one minute of gentle exercise, count your breaths again for one minute. This is your breathing rate after exercise.

Make a table from your results.

That's 26 breaths in one minute.

After one minute of exercise I will count how many times I breathe in for one minute.

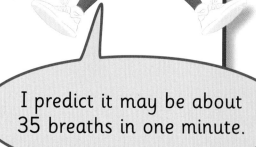

I predict it may be about 35 breaths in one minute.

My prediction of breaths in one minute at rest	My prediction of breaths in one minute after exercise	Number of breaths in one minute at rest	Number of breaths in one minute after exercise

Were your predictions right?

Investigating breathing rates

Sofia and Marcus tested the breaths per minute of two teachers.
They recorded the results in this table.

Person	Age	Prediction At rest	Breathing Rate at Rest	Prediction after exercise	Breathing Rate after Exercise
Sofia	11	20	26	40	50
Marcus	11	35	27	45	48
Mr. Zan	31	30	23	40	41
Mrs. Bell	29	25	24	35	39

Questions

1   Why does the breathing rate per minute always
    increase after exercise?

2   Whose breathing rate per minute increased most?

3   Why was the breathing rate per minute of the adults
    lower than that of the children?

Your stomach and intestines

When you eat, your food goes to your stomach and
intestines. Your intestines absorb important nutrients
from your food. Nutrients are things in your food
that help your body to grow and work well.
Nutrients help to keep you healthy.

The food then passes out of your intestines
and into the toilet as waste.

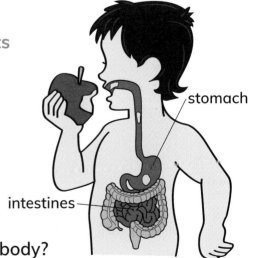

stomach

intestines

Question

4   What organ makes the blood travel around your body?

Your brain

Like your heart, your brain never stops working. Your brain gets messages from your sense organs, your eyes, ears, tongue, skin and nose. Your brain uses that information when you think, talk, write and move. This helps you talk, write, do mathematics, play games and more. You need your brain for everything you do!

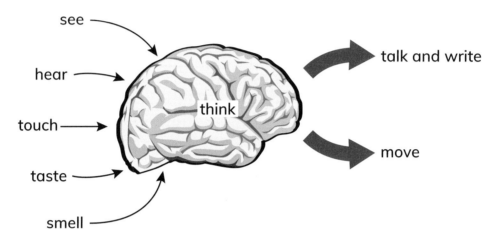

If you make your brain work hard it gets better. Scientists know that, even when you get things wrong, if you keep trying your brain will improve.

Questions

5   Can you remember a time when you had to think very hard?

6   Do you know a game that makes your brain work hard?

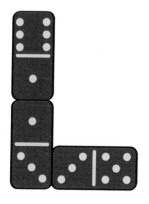 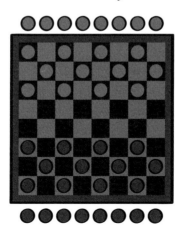 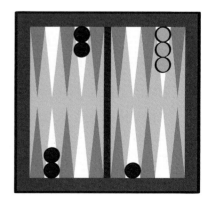

Activity 1

Exercising your brain!

You will need: paper and pencil

Play a game of noughts and crosses with a friend.

Did the game make you think?
To win you have to think hard.

Now think of a way to make the game better. Could you have three players? or a 4 × 4 grid?

Work out how to play the new game.

Show the new game to your friends.

Did this make your brain work?

Have you tried some new ideas?

Did you feel your brain working hard?

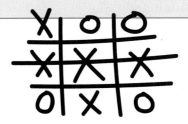

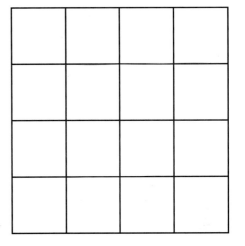

Activity 2

Organ quiz

You will need: paper, scissors, pens

Cut a sheet of paper into four pieces. On each piece, draw one of these body organs: the heart, lungs, brain, stomach and intestines. Turn each piece of paper over. Ask a friend to choose one, which they then show to you. You have to say the name of the organ and tell them what the organ does. Then write this on the back of the paper.

Take it in turns to do the rest. Did you both get them right?

When you learn things about the human body, does it make you want to know more?
Why is this?

Look what I can do!

- ☐ I know about some of the important organs in humans.
- ☐ I can say what these body organs do.
- ☐ I can think and talk about results recorded on a bar chart and look for patterns in these results.
- ☐ I can make a conclusion from results
- ☐ I can make predictions and see if they were right.
- ☐ I can record information in a table.

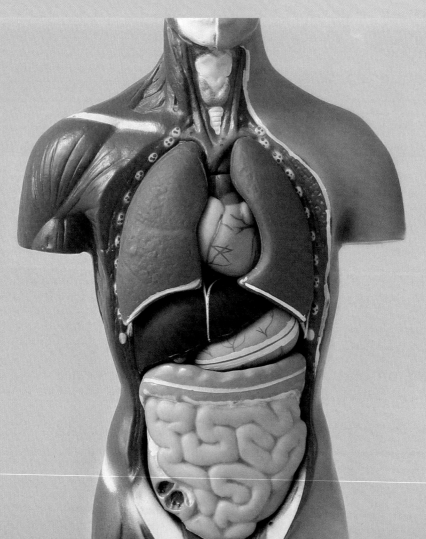

> 4.2 Animal groups and different life cycles

We are going to:

- recognise the different body parts of different groups of animals
- describe and compare the different life cycles of different animals
- use observations to sort animals into different groups
- use a diagram to show how life cycles work
- use a bar chart to answer questions
- use information sources to research and answer questions.

Getting started

- What is happening in the picture?
- What will happen next in the life of this animal?
- What body parts can you see on this animal?

amphibian
baby
caterpillar
cold-blooded
hatch
life cycle
mammal
reptile
tadpole
warm-blooded

Scientists put animals into groups

Animals have many body parts. Some are similar like eyes, some are quite different like claws or horns.

Some animals are warm-blooded because their bodies make heat inside. Others are cold-blooded. Their bodies are the same temperature as their environment around them.

Scientists put animals into groups. Here are six of the groups that scientists use.

Group	
mammals (warm-blooded, body hair, they have **babies**)	
reptiles (cold-blooded, scales, lay eggs)	
fish (cold-blooded, gills, scales, live in water, lay eggs)	
birds (warm-blooded, feathers, lay eggs)	
insects (body in three parts, six legs, lay eggs)	
amphibians (live on land and in water, cold-blooded, lay eggs)	

Questions

1 Look at the animals shown in the table.
  Point to their different body parts.

2 Think of another animal for each group.

3 In which group would you put humans?

Activity 1

Six groups of animals

You will need: slips of paper or sticky notes, pens

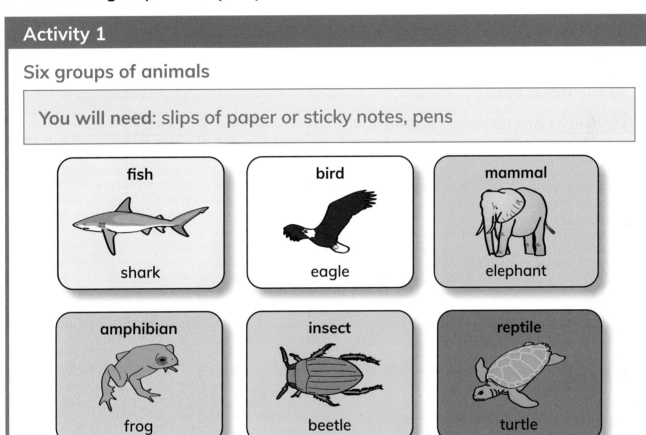

With a friend, make six animal group cards like these.

On 10 bits of paper write 10 names of different animals (include at least one mammal, one reptile, one fish, one bird, one insect, one amphibian).

Take turns to place each name with the correct animal group card.

Now join with others in your class and add their animals to your groups.

Some animals may be harder to group, so you will need to think and talk about them. It may help to look in a book.

Adult animals and their young

All young animals start life smaller than the adults. Some look like their parents. These polar bears are mammals.

Questions

4 How is the baby bear similar to the adult bear?

5 Do they both have the same body parts?

Some young animals look different to their parents.

Look at these insects. Can you see the young butterfly we call a caterpillar and the adult butterfly?

Question

6 How is the caterpillar different to the adult?

Life cycles

All animals grow through different parts of their life. The body of the animal changes. Animals always start life as an egg or a baby. When they are adults, animals can make new eggs or babies.

These changes happen one after another. Changes happen from the start of the animal's life and go on until the end of its life. We call this the animal's life cycle.

Look at the life cycle of the chicken from egg to adult. We can follow the arrows from change to change.

Each life cycle diagram is a model which helps us learn.

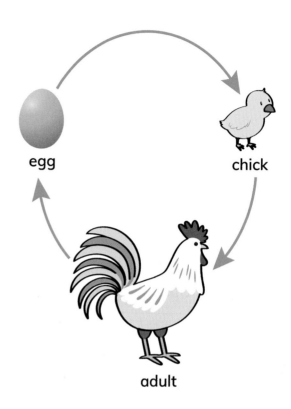

egg

chick

adult

Question

7   How does the chicken's body change from chick to adult?

As a child you have changed since you were a baby.
The life cycle of a human includes these five stages.

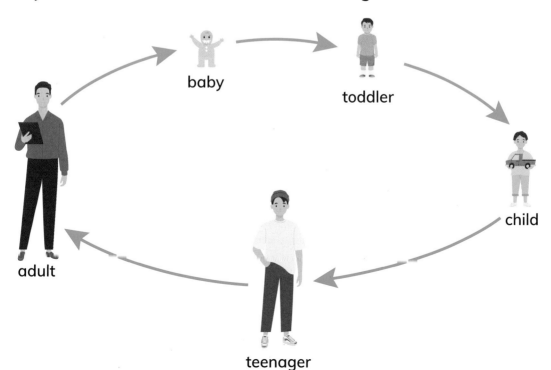

baby

toddler

child

teenager

adult

Activity 2

Changes as we grow

> **You will need:** a picture of a baby, a female child, a male adult and an elderly woman, paper, pen

Look at the pictures of a human life cycle. Talk about the differences between a baby and a child. Think about size, hair, teeth and other things.

List three things that change as a person grows older.

Talk about things that don't change as you grow up.

Draw a picture of yourself as a grown up.

Life cycle of a frog

In humans the baby looks similar to the adult.

The young of frogs look very different to the adults.

Frogs lay eggs which hatch into tadpoles. Young tadpoles have a body and a tail. The tadpoles slowly grow legs and lose their tails. They begin to look like small frogs and we call them froglets.

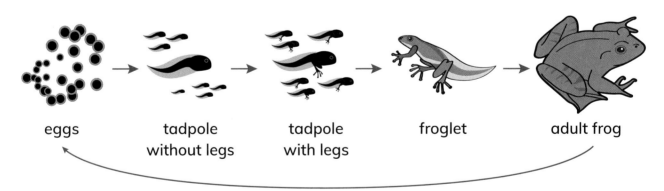

| eggs | tadpole without legs | tadpole with legs | froglet | adult frog |

Activity 3

Drawing the life cycle of the frog

You will need: paper, pen

Look at the pictures which show how a frog changes from egg to tadpole and tadpole to frog.

Draw pictures and use arrows to draw the life cycle of a frog. Include these words to label the stages: eggs, tadpole, tadpole with legs, froglet, adult.

Talk about how the life cycle of the frog is different to the life cycle of a human.

Think like a scientist

Height increases from baby to child

As each human grows their height changes. Look at this bar chart of a child's height each birthday from one to ten years old.

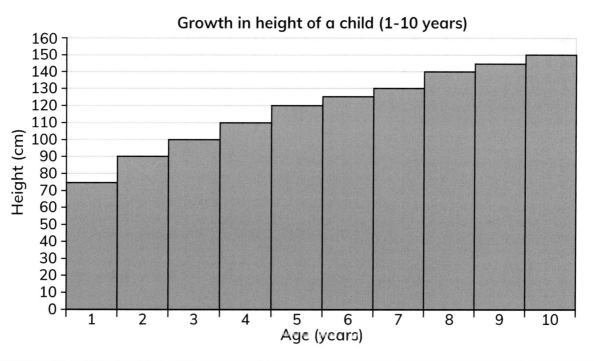

Growth in height of a child (1-10 years)

Continued

Answer these questions.

1 What was the child's height at 2 years old?
2 From age 1 to 2 years how much did the child's height increase?
3 From age 9 to 10 years how much did the child's height increase?
4 Why might a doctor or parent might be pleased to see this graph?

How am I doing?

Look at the graph on the previous page. What is the pattern?
What does the whole graph tell us?

A life cycle diagram helps us to see changes over time.
How do these diagrams help you learn about science?

Look what I can do!

☐ I can recognise the different body parts of different groups of animals.
☐ I can describe and compare the different life cycles of different animals.
☐ I can use observations to sort animals into different groups.
☐ I can use a diagram to show how life cycles work.
☐ I can use a bar chart to answer questions.
☐ I can use information sources to research and answer questions.

> 4.3 Food chains

We are going to:

- read, talk about, draw and write food chains
- learn that in a food chain the plant is the producer and the animals are consumers
- use a diagram to show the steps in a food chain
- make a prediction about what might happen to a food chain
- use information sources to research and answer questions.

Getting started

Look at the picture.

What do the different fish like to eat?

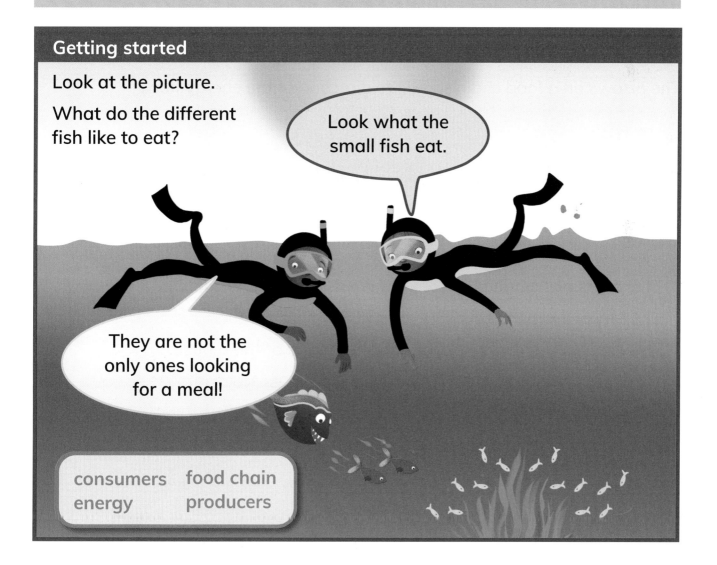

consumers   food chain
energy   producers

Zara and Arun are in the sea, observing fish and what they eat. They can see that the seaweeds grow in the sunlight. Seaweeds make their own food using sunlight. Seaweed are producers because they use sunlight to make their own food.

Animals are consumers because they have to eat other living things to get their energy. Energy from food means you can grow and move. Every part of your body needs energy to make it work and grow.

In different environments around the world, different animals eat different things. Some animals eat only plants. Other animals eat animals. Some animals eat plants and animals.

We show all this on a diagram. We call it a food chain. A food chain shows us how different living things need other living things for food.

The arrows on a food chain show the direction of the energy flow.

Question

1 Name some animals that only eat plants.

Activity 1

Food for a mouse and a cat

The seeds are made by a corn plant using the Sun's energy.

The mouse eats the seeds.

The energy from the seed goes into the body of the mouse.

If a cat eats the mouse, the energy in the mouse goes into the body of the cat.

Continued

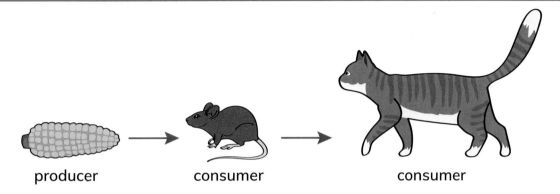

producer   consumer   consumer

Copy this food chain.
Make sure the arrows show the direction of the energy.

Why is corn the producer? Why are the mouse and cat consumers?

A food chain can include pictures.
We can do the same with words and arrows, like this.

corn ➡ mouse ➡ cat

Activity 2

Drawing a food chain

Look at the environment shown by the picture. Draw a food chain for this environment and then write it out in words. Start with a plant and draw in different consumers. Make sure you draw the arrows the right way around.

A food chain is a model which helps us understand how living things get energy.

Think like a scientist

Animals need other living things

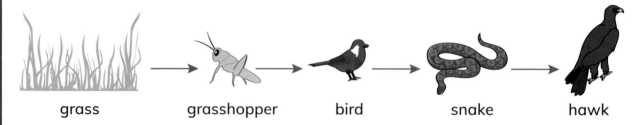

grass   grasshopper   bird   snake   hawk

Look at this food chain. Observe how the arrows show the energy moving from living thing to living thing. Draw this food chain using words and arrows only.

Now answer these questions.

1   If there was no grass what would happen?
2   If the weather was very cold and the snakes all hid underground, what might happen to the hawks?

How am I doing?

Some humans eat goat meat. Draw a food chain beginning with a producer and include a goat and a human.

Science helps us to look at living things in new ways. We know plants are needed for all life on Earth. How has science made you think differently about things like plants?

Look what I can do!

- ☐ I can read, talk about, draw and write food chains.
- ☐ I know that in a food chain the plant is the producer and the animals are consumers.
- ☐ I can use a diagram to show the steps in a food chain.
- ☐ I can make a prediction about what might happen to a food chain.
- ☐ I can use information sources to research and answer questions.

> 4.4 Fossils

We are going to:

- explore how fossils are impressions, or remains of things that were once alive
- make and use models in science
- use information sources to research and answer questions.

Getting started

Look at this pattern of an animal which lived about 150 million years ago.

- What body parts can you see?
- How was this pattern made?

fossil   gum   impression

Fossils

The pattern in the rock shown by the photo is the fossil of this animal, a flying reptile called a Pterodactyl.

The animal had a long beak, a long neck, claws on its wings and two feet. All Pterodactyl died a very long time ago. But scientists have found many fossils of these animals in rocks.

A fossil is an impression made in mud. The hard parts of the dead animal press into the mud, and the shape of the hard parts is copied in the mud. Over a long time, the mud turns to rock.

Activity 1

So many fossils

> **You will need:** fossils, photographs of fossils, magnifying glasses

Look at the photographs of different fossils on the next page.
One shows the first bird, Archaeopteryx.
Can you see its body parts? Can you see its feathers?

Continued

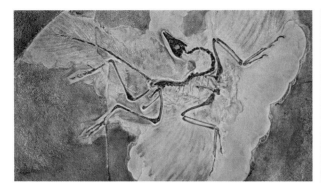

A fossil bird

A fossil fish

A fossil dragonfly

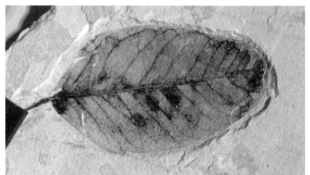

A fossil leaf

Fossil dinosaur eggs

Use a magnifying glass to look at some fossils or these photographs.
Can you see the parts of the animal or plant? Draw one of the fossils and
write notes to say what it is. How do you think the fossil was made?

Activity 2

Make a fossil!

You will need: modelling clay, a shell, plaster, newspaper

Make your own fossil by pressing a shell into clay to make an impression. Fill the impression with plaster and let it dry. Then pull out the dry plaster shaped like a shell.

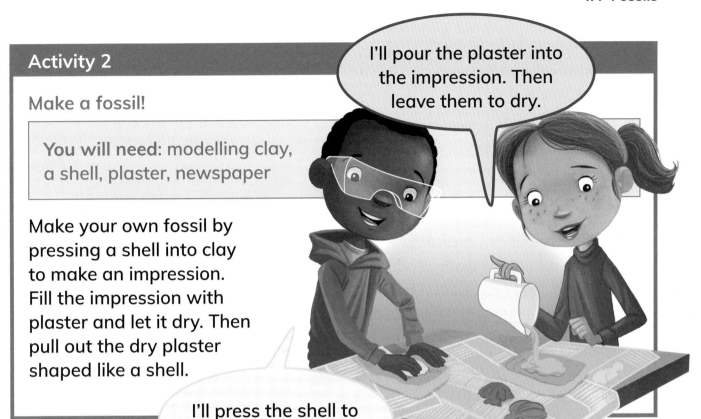

Scientists who find fossils

Most fossils are buried under rocks deep underground. Sometimes the sea or a river will wash the rock away so that the fossil is easy to find. If scientists find a fossil, they dig it up very carefully.

These pictures show how a fossil formed deep in the ground can appear at the surface.

fossil

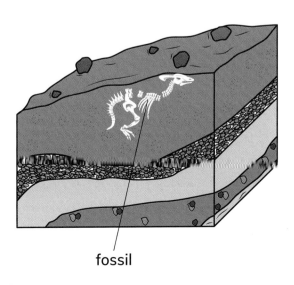

fossil

117

Think like a scientist 1

Make a fossil dig

You will need: a large tray or box, sand, shells or fossils, a trowel, paintbrushes, a magnifying glass

When scientists dig for fossils they must be very careful. The fossils must not be damaged. This is why they use small tools and even paintbrushes to brush away soil and sand.

Can you find the buried fossils in your sand tray? Try to do this without damaging them.

A different type of fossil

Some fossils are different. This insect was trapped many years ago in sticky tree gum. Now we can see it very clearly as a fossil insect.

Think like a scientist 2

Finding out about Mary Anning

You will need: books about fossils, the internet

Over 200 years ago, Mary Anning lived by the sea in England. Mary collected fossils and became famous as a fossil collector. Below is a photograph of the fossil she discovered. At that time most scientists were men.

Have a look in books and on the internet for information about Mary Anning, her father, and her dog, Tray.

With a friend make a poster about Mary's fossil collecting, include three or four interesting things about her life.

What kind of science enquiry skills are you using here?

How am I doing?

Why did Mary Anning become famous?

How could you study living things in your local environment?

If you become a scientist, what would you study?

Check your progress

Talk about the answers to these questions with your class.

1 Name the human organs below.

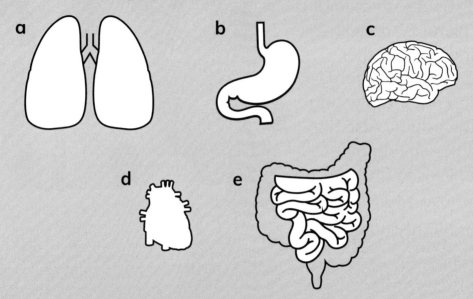

2 Say which group each animal belongs to.
Choose from these groups.

mammal   reptile   insect   amphibian   fish   bird

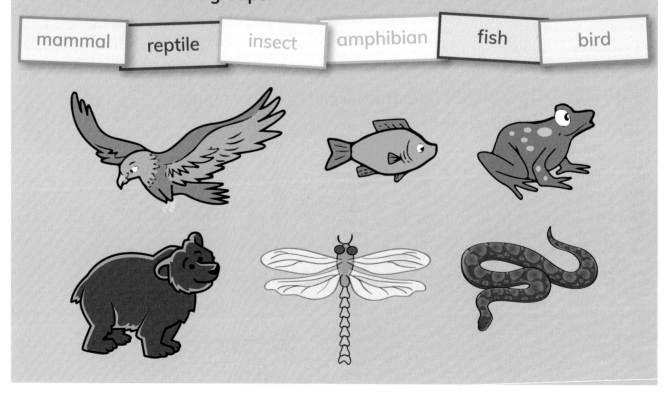

Continued

3   Look at this life cycle of a frog. Then answer the
    questions below.

   a   Which stage follows the tadpole without legs?
   b   Which stage follows the small frog with a tail?
   c   In what two ways is the frog different from the
       tadpole without legs?

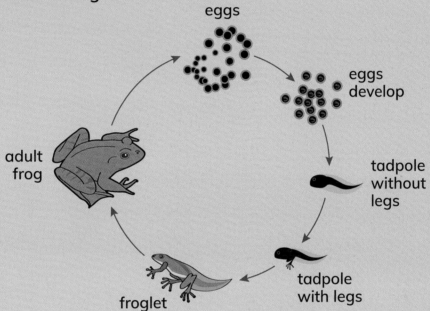

4   Draw a food chain including three or more of these living things.

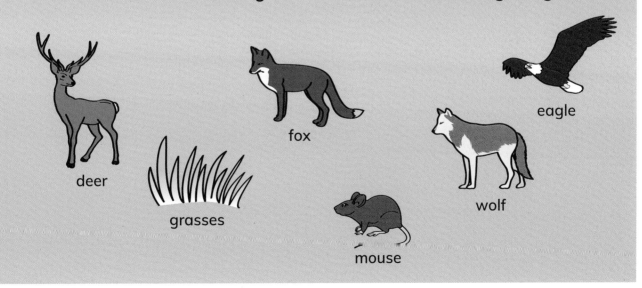

Continued

5 Look at this fossil. Then answer the questions.

a Did this animal live on land or in the water?

b Explain why you think so.

c What features of the animal can you see in the fossil?

d What is a fossil?

Select A, B or C.

A. A fossil is the real animal.

B. A fossil is an impression made in rock.

C. A fossil is a model made by scientists.

5 > Forces and magnets

> 5.1 Forces and forcemeters

We are going to:

- measure forces using a forcemeter

- measure using standard units

- compare standard and non-standard units

- make a bar chart of results

- learn how the science of forces was different in the past.

Getting started

Forces are pushes and pulls.

- Look at the children on this rollercoaster. Talk with a friend about the forces you might feel at a fairground.

- Forces can make things happen. Write down some different types of changes that happen because of forces.

forcemeter   newton   non-standard units

gravity   standard units   weight

Our understanding of forces was different in the past.

Here are three scientists who changed the science of forces.

John Philoponus, lived in Egypt, 490–580

Philoponus wrote that objects move because making them move gives them a force.

Ibn Sina, lived in Iran, 980–1037

Ibn Sina worked out that forces can make objects move.

Isaac Newton, lived in Great Britain, 1643–1727

Newton found out that forces can make objects speed up, slow down or change direction.

Scientists now know a lot about forces.

Forces can make some objects change shape.

They can make objects speed up, slow down or change direction.

Mae Jemison was a scientist who investigated forces in space.

Gravity is the force that pulls objects towards the Earth. Gravity makes object have weight. Weight is another force you can measure.

Think like a scientist 1

Make a simple forcemeter

You will need: a rubber band, two paper clips, a piece of cardboard, glue and a piece of lined paper

A forcemeter is a piece of equipment we use to measure the strength of a force. Zara has made a simple forcemeter.

Make a forcemeter like this.

Mark the end of the rubber band. Label this zero.

Then number each line below the zero mark.

Use your forcemeter to measure some forces.

Continued

You can measure the force needed to pull things.
A force of 11 lines is needed to make this book move.

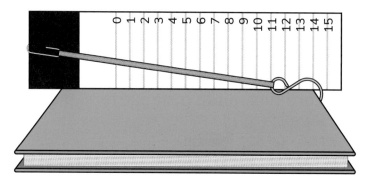

These scissors have a weight of 8 lines.

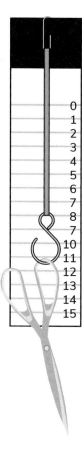

Measure some different forces and make a table of your results.

Standard units and forcemeters

Standard units are useful for measuring.

Metres (m) and centimetres (cm) are standard units of length.

Minutes (min) and seconds (s) are standard units of time.

Standard units are useful because everyone in the world who uses them can compare their measurements.

The standard unit of force is the newton (N). This unit is named after the scientist Isaac Newton. This forcemeter can measure in newtons.

Questions

1 Name a force you can measure.

2 What is the standard unit of force?

3 Why are standard units better than non-standard units?

Think like a scientist 2

Make a better forcemeter

You will need: your simple forcemeter, some plain paper, some glue and some 100 g masses

The simple forcemeter uses lines as a unit of force. It uses a non-standard unit.

You can make a better forcemeter by making it measure in standard units, newtons.

On Earth, a 100 gram (100 g) mass has a weight of 1 newton (1 N).

Zara uses this fact to make her forcemeter better.

Continued

Zara adds a new piece of paper and marks the zero line.

Then she hangs a 100 g mass on her forcemeter and marks the 1 newton line.

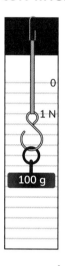

Then she adds another 100 g mass and marks the 2 newton line. She marks halfway between each line so she can measure half newtons.

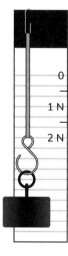

Make your forcemeter measure in newtons. Then use it to measure some forces.

Make a bar chart to show your results.

Continued

Use your forcemeter to check a friend's results. If you get a different answer, you should both measure again very carefully to check what the right answer is.

Which of the forcemeters you used is better?
How does making a forcemeter help you to learn about forces?

Look what I can do!

☐ I can measure forces using a forcemeter.

☐ I can measure using standard units.

☐ I can say why standard units are better than non-standard units.

☐ I can make a bar chart of results.

☐ I can explain how the science of forces was different in the past.

> 5.2 Gravity

We are going to:

- learn about the force of gravity
- measure using standard units
- choose the best equipment and use it correctly
- make predictions and say whether they are correct or not
- do an investigation safely.

Getting started

Look at this picture of the Earth.

- Talk to a friend about the countries you can see.
- Why do people living in countries near the bottom of this picture not **fall** off the Earth?

fall

Which way is down?

The Earth's gravity is a force that pulls objects towards the centre of the Earth. When we drop things, they fall down. Down is a different direction in different places on the Earth. Down is always towards the centre of the Earth.

People and objects do not fall off the Earth because they can only fall towards the centre of the Earth. Gravity makes things have weight.

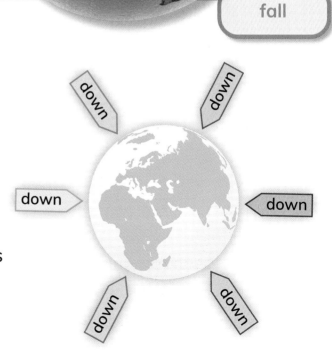

Questions

1. In which direction do things fall?
2. What is the force that pulls things towards the centre of the Earth?
3. Why do things not fall off the Earth?

Activity

Draw a picture of falling

> **You will need:** paper and a pencil

Draw a picture of the Earth. Draw some pictures of things that fall in different places around the Earth. Make sure the things you draw are all falling in the right direction.

Think like a scientist

Do heavier objects fall faster?

> **You will need:** some objects, some forcemeters and a cushion

Arun makes some predictions about what will happen when these objects fall.

Zara disagrees. She has a different prediction.

Tell a friend what you think will happen.

Give a reason for your prediction.

The empty bottle will fall faster because it is smaller.

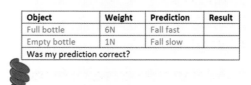

Object	Weight	Prediction	Result
Full bottle	6N	Fall fast	
Empty bottle	1N	Fall slow	
Was my prediction correct?			

Choose the best forcemeter to measure the weight of each object.

Predict what will happen when they fall.

Continued

Write your measurements and predictions in a table like Arun's.

What will you need to keep the same to make this a fair test?

Test how your objects fall and check by dropping them again.

How can you stay safe in this investigation? Why is the cushion useful?

Write the results in your table.

Record whether your prediction was correct.

How am I doing?

Talk to your classmates about what they found out.
Were their predictions correct?

Compare your results. Is there a pattern in the results?
Do heavier objects fall faster?

When your predictions are not correct, it means you have learned something new.
Tell a friend what you think Arun and Zara learned from their investigation.

Look what I can do!

- ☐ I can explain what gravity does.
- ☐ I can measure in newtons.
- ☐ I can choose the best equipment and use it correctly.
- ☐ I can say whether my predictions are correct or not.
- ☐ I can do practical work safely.

> 5.3 Friction

We are going to:

- learn where friction happens and what it does

- measure friction on rough and smooth surfaces using a forcemeter

- ask a scientific question, then plan a scientific enquiry to find the answer

- choose the best equipment and use it correctly

- link our conclusion to our scientific question.

Getting started

Look at these slides.

- How are they different?

- Which do you think is best?

- What would the best slide in the world look like? Draw a picture of your ideas.

- How could you make your slide really fast?

| friction | slippery |
| grip | surface |

What is friction?

When one object moves on another object it makes a force called friction.

Friction happens where the outside part of the object, the surface, pushes over the surface of the other object.

The friction pushes against the movement, so it slows down the moving object.

Gravity is pulling this girl down the slide. Friction between the surface of her clothes and the surface of the slide slows her down. The more friction there is the slower she will slide.

Sometimes we use the word grip to describe friction. A surface that has lots of friction has good grip and can be called a grippy surface.
A surface that only has a little friction is called a slippery surface.

friction

gravity

Rub your hands together.
Friction can make your hands warm.

Too much friction can burn your skin.

Questions

1 What does friction do to moving objects?

2 Where does the friction happen?

3 Why do you move so fast on a water slide?

Think like a scientist 1

Which surface has the least friction?

You will need: some forcemeters, an object to pull, some different surfaces

Pull your object over different surfaces and choose a forcemeter to measure the friction.

Try using a very smooth surface and a very rough surface. Predict which surface will have the least friction.

Record your measurements in a table of results. Use your results to make a conclusion.

How am I doing?

Read your conclusion. It should give the answer to the question you are investigating: *Which surface has the least friction?*

Does your conclusion answer this question?
If it does not, write a better conclusion.

Think like a scientist 2

Questions about friction

You will need: a forcemeter, some masses, some water, some shoes or other objects to pull

Zara and Arun have a new question about friction. What type of scientific enquiry can they do to find out the answer: research, pattern seeking, observing changes over time, fair testing or identification and classification?

> 5.4 Amazing magnets

We are going to:

- learn about the poles of magnets and what they do
- look for patterns in our results
- learn about some uses of magnets.

Getting started

This game uses magnets.

- Draw a picture of some different types of magnets.
- Label the picture to show what you know about magnets.

attract   magnetism   north pole   repel   south pole

Magnets and poles

Magnets come in different shapes.

All magnets have a north pole and a south pole. The north pole is sometimes coloured red and the south pole coloured blue.

Magnets can push and pull. This force is called magnetism. Materials that are pulled towards a magnet are magnetic materials. The metal paper clips shown below are magnetic. The magnet attracts the paper clips. Materials that are not attracted to a magnet are non-magnetic materials.

Sometimes magnets can push apart instead of pulling together. Magnets can repel.

Repel is the opposite of attract.

bar magnet

horseshoe magnet

fridge magnet

Think like a scientist

Investigating poles

You will need: some magnets and some magnetic and non-magnetic objects

I think a north pole always attracts

Sofia and Arun are trying to work out when the poles of magnets attract and when they repel.

Use your magnets to find out. Look for patterns in what happens. Does the same thing happen every time? How far apart do the magnets need to be?

Is Arun's idea correct?
Write some sentences to show what you find out.

How am I doing?

Have a look at a friend's sentences.
Use the magnets to check whether their sentences are correct.
Tell your friend what you find out.

Magnets attract, magnets repel

Opposite poles will always attract each other.

Two poles the same will always repel each other.

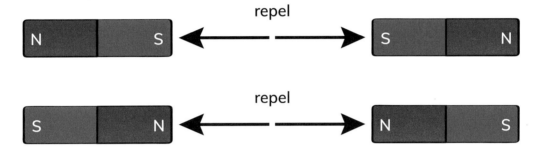

North poles and south poles both attract magnetic materials.

Questions

1 What are the two poles of a magnet called?

2 Which pole is blue, and which is red?

3 Do all magnets have poles?

What are magnets used for?

Magnets have many uses.

This crane is using a magnet to sort metal.

A wind turbine uses magnets to make electricity.

An electric motor uses magnets to make things move.

Activity

How do we use magnets?

You will need: poster paper and pens

Work with a friend to explain how something uses magnets. Draw a large picture of your object and add a title. Write down at least two sentences to say to your class. Practise your sentences, then present your object to the class.

An electric scooter uses magnets.

ELECTRIC SCOOTER

The magnets are in the electric motor tha makes the scooter mov

Look what I can do!

☐ I can describe the poles of a magnet and explain what they do.

☐ I can describe a pattern in my results.

☐ I can explain how magnets make something work.

> 5.5 Magnetic materials

We are going to:

- **investigate which materials are magnetic**
- **find out which types of scientific enquiry we are using**
- **make predictions and compare them with our results**
- **use patterns in results to make conclusions.**

Getting started

- Make a list of the materials that you think magnets are attracted to.
- Swap your list with a friend.
  Tell them whether you agree with their list.

Magnetic or non-magnetic?

Sofia and Arun are using magnets to pull toy cars. Sofia's car is not moving. Why?

Sofia's car is not attracted to the magnet because it is made of wood. Wood is a non-magnetic material. Arun's car is made of a metal called steel. Steel is magnetic.

Questions

1   Name a magnetic material.

2   Name a non-magnetic material.

3   Why didn't Sofia's car move?

Think like a scientist 1

Predicting which materials are magnetic

You will need: a magnet and some different materials to test

- Predict which materials will be magnetic.
- Then test the materials to see whether you were right.

There are five types of scientific enquiry: research, fair testing, observing over time, identifying and classifying, or pattern seeking. This is a classifying enquiry. You will classify the materials by whether they are magnetic or non-magnetic.

Continued

- Write your predictions and results in a table like this.

Object	Material	Prediction	Result
plastic bottle	plastic	non-magnetic	non-magnetic

Were your predictions correct?

You can also use pattern seeking in the investigation.

- Make a new table like this to classify the materials.

It will make it easier to see the pattern.

Magnetic materials	Non-magnetic materials
	wood

Can you see the pattern in your results now?

What types of materials are magnetic?

- Use the pattern to write a conclusion.
  Make sure it gives the answer to the investigation question.

Was it easier to find the pattern when you classified the materials into two groups?

Often it is easier to find patterns if you present your results in a different way.

For some results, a chart or graph can help you to see any patterns.

Think like a scientist 2

Which metals are magnetic?

You will need: some samples of different metals and a magnet

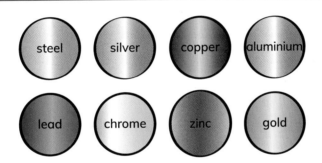

Predict which metals will be magnetic and which will be non-magnetic.

Record your predictions and results in a table like this.

Metal	Prediction	Result
Steel	magnetic	magnetic
Aluminium	magnetic	non-magnetic

Continued

Which type of scientific enquiry is this: research, fair testing, observing over time, identifying and classifying, or pattern seeking?

Were your predictions correct?

Use your results to write a conclusion.
Make sure it gives the answer to the investigation question.

How am I doing?

Share your results with a friend.
Do you have the same result for each metal?

If not, you will both need to test that metal again.

Look what I can do!

- ☐ I can name some magnetic and some non-magnetic materials.
- ☐ I can give an example of a scientific enquiry that uses pattern seeking.
- ☐ I can give an example of a scientific enquiry that uses classification.
- ☐ I can use my results to say whether my prediction was correct.
- ☐ I can use a pattern in results to make a conclusion.

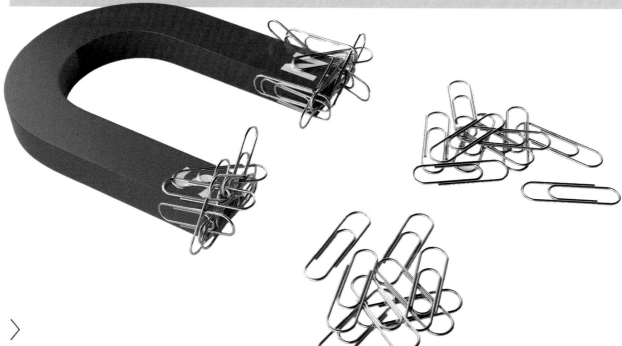

Project: How friction helps us

Zara loves to run.

She makes a poster to show how friction helps her when she is running.

She has prepared a short talk for her friends to explain what would happen if there was no friction when she was running.

If there was no friction, I would not be able to stop.

Friction and Running

Friction stops shoelaces coming undone

Grip

Good friction on the track

What do you like to do?

Make a poster showing how friction helps you do it.

Prepare a short talk to explain what would happen if you tried to do it and there was no friction.

Present your poster and your short talk to your class.

Check your progress

Talk about the answers to these questions with your class.

1 Which forcemeter is measuring the greatest force?

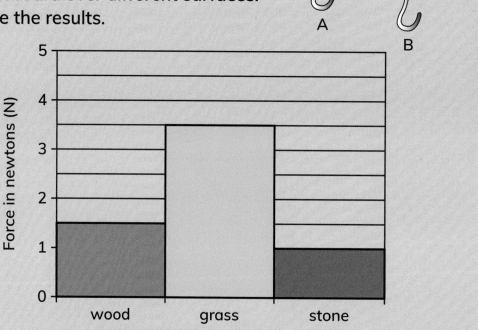

2 Alex tested the force needed to pull his skateboard over different surfaces. Here are the results.

a Which surface had the most friction?

b Which surface had the least friction?

c How much more friction was there on the wood than on the stone?

Continued

3 What would happen if a magnet was put close to this metal toy car?

4 Which of these objects is magnetic and which is non-magnetic?

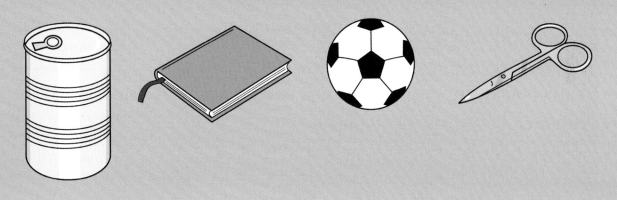

The shape of the Earth, Sun and Moon

The Earth, the Sun and the Moon are all spheres.
The same shape as a ball. We can say they are spherical.

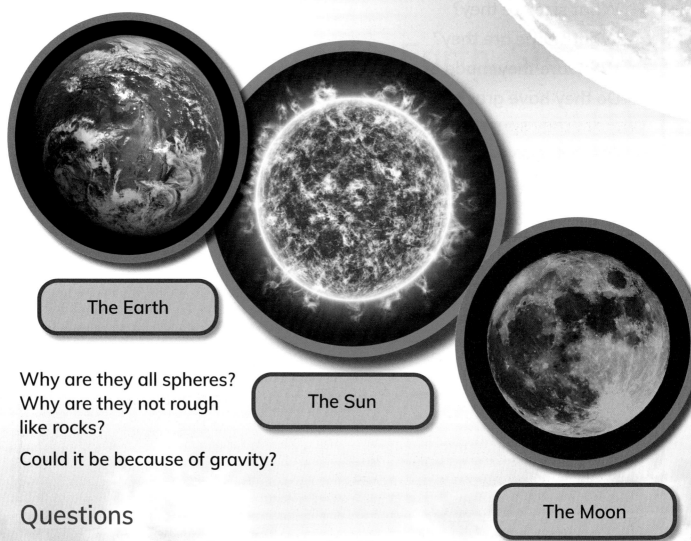

The Earth

The Sun

The Moon

Why are they all spheres?
Why are they not rough like rocks?

Could it be because of gravity?

Questions

1 Can you name the five types of scientific enquiry?

2 Which of them can you use to find out more about the Earth, Sun and Moon?

Think like a scientist

Researching the Earth, Sun and Moon

You will need: books, videos or websites about the Earth, Sun and Moon

What can you find out about the Earth, Sun and Moon?

Why are they spheres?

Do they all have gravity?

Are they the same size?

Write these and some of your own questions on a piece of paper.

Use books, videos or the internet to find out the answers to as many of the questions as you can.

How am I doing?

Have a look at a friend's questions.
Can you help them with the answers?

Can they help you with yours?

Which do you like using best: books, videos or the internet?
Think of one thing that is good about each of them.
Think of one thing that is not good about each of them.

Gravity makes spheres

The Earth, the Sun and the Moon are all spheres because of gravity.

Every object with mass has gravity. The more mass an object has the stronger the gravity.

The Moon is smaller than the Earth, so the Moon's gravity is weaker than Earth's.

The Sun is much bigger than the Earth, so the Sun's gravity is much stronger than Earth's.

An object's gravity pulls everything towards the centre of the object.

The Earth is a sphere because the Earth's gravity pulls everything, even itself, towards the centre.

The Moon is a sphere because the Moon's gravity pulls all the rock it is made of towards the centre.

The Sun is a sphere because the Sun's gravity pulls all the gas it is made of towards the centre.

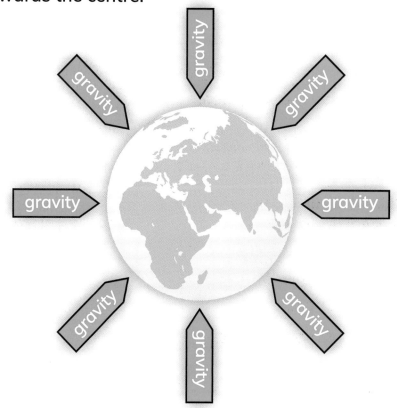

Activity

Modelling gravity

You will need: a piece of clay

Scientists often use models to find out how things work.

A diagram can be a type of model because it can show how something works.

We can also make 3D models to find things out.

Arun is using clay to model how gravity makes things into spheres.

Each time he turns the clay he uses his hands to push towards the centre.

Try doing this with a piece of clay.

Start with a piece that is not a sphere.

Try to push with the same force each time.

If you do this carefully for long enough you will shape your clay into a sphere.

Now answer these questions.

1 In this model, what shows the Earth?

2 In this model, what does the force from your hands do?

3 Describe one way this model is different from how gravity really shaped the Earth.

4 Name two types of models that scientists use.

Push ⟶   ⟵ Push

Facts about the Moon

The Moon is a large sphere of rock that is moving slowly in a circle around the Earth. We call this circle the Moon's orbit. The Moon takes 29 days to orbit the Earth.

The Moon has many craters. Craters are made when space rocks hit the Moon's surface.

The Moon is the only place in space that humans have ever been. Neil Armstrong was the first person to walk on the Moon in 1969.

Questions

1 What shape is the Moon's orbit?

2 How long does the Moon take to orbit the Earth?

3 Why does the Moon have craters?

Think like a scientist 1

Modelling the Moon's orbit

You will need: some paper, a piece of string, some sticky tape and a large space

Sofia has squashed some paper to make a ball. She has used sticky tape to fix some string to the paper ball. She is using the ball to show how the Moon orbits the Earth.

Try modelling the Moon's orbit like Sofia.

Make sure you do not hit anyone with the paper ball.

Continued

The Moon is moving fast but it orbits the Earth because gravity always pulls it towards the Earth. The string is being gravity in this model.

Answer these questions.

1 How can you stay safe in this activity?
2 What is being the Moon in this model?
3 What is being the Earth in this model?

Think like a scientist 2

Making a scale model

> **You will need:** some white paper, colour pencils, 385 cm of string, a ruler and a large space

A scale model is a model that shows things at the correct size compared to each other. We can make a scale model of the Earth and the Moon. The model will show how big the Moon is compared to the Earth and how far away it is in space.

In our scale model we will draw every 1000 km as 1 cm.

The Earth is about 13 000 km across. In the model it will be 13 cm.

The Moon is about 3500 km across. In the model it will be 3.5 cm.

The Moon is about 385 000 km away from Earth.
In the model it will be 385 cm away.

Continued

- First draw a circle 13 cm across on white paper.

- Then colour it to look like the Earth and cut it out.

- Next draw a circle 3.5 cm across on white paper.

- Then draw some craters so it looks like the Moon and cut it out.

- Now put your model Earth on the floor.

- Use the string to measure 385 cm away from the Earth and put the Moon there.

- Finally, stand back and look at your model.

Does the Moon look close to the Earth or far away?

It took astronauts three days to travel to the Moon in a rocket.

This is a real photograph of the Earth and Moon taken from a spacecraft called OSIRIS-Rex. It was five million kilometres away when it took the photo. Your model should look like this.

Continued

How am I doing?

Compare your model with a model made by two other people in your class. Do they look the same?

If they look different, check all the measurements.

Some models show how things work.
Other models show how things look.
You have used two models in this topic.
Which model showed how something worked?
Which model showed how something looked?

Look what I can do!

☐   I can describe the movement of the Moon.

☐   I can learn science from different types of model.

> 6.3 The phases of the Moon

We are going to:

- learn why the Moon appears to change shape
- learn why the Moon appears to move across the sky by describing the movement of the Earth and Moon
- make a model to show why the Moon appears to change shape
- record observations in a table.

Getting started

- Draw a picture of the Moon.
- Compare your picture with your friends' pictures.
- How many different shaped moons can you see?
- What shape is the Moon? Tell your friends what you think.

crescent	rotate
gibbous	southern hemisphere
northern hemisphere	waning
phase	waxing

The phases of the Moon

In space, light from the Sun only shines on the front half of the Moon. Looking at the Moon from Earth, we often see some of the dark half of the Moon. It looks as though the Moon changes shape. The different shapes are called phases.

When the Moon is further away from the Sun than Earth, we see lots of the light side and only a little of the dark side. This phase is called a gibbous Moon.

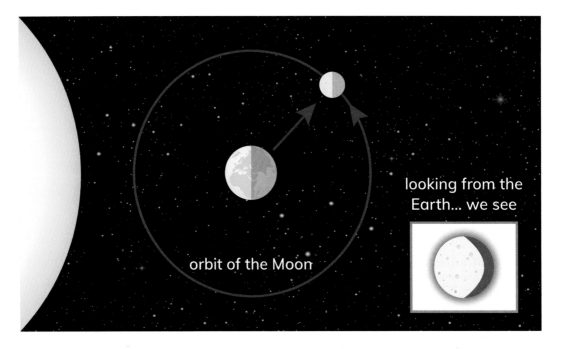

orbit of the Moon

looking from the Earth... we see

When the Moon is the same distance away from the Sun as Earth, we see half of each side. This phase is called a first quarter moon because it is a quarter of the way around its orbit.

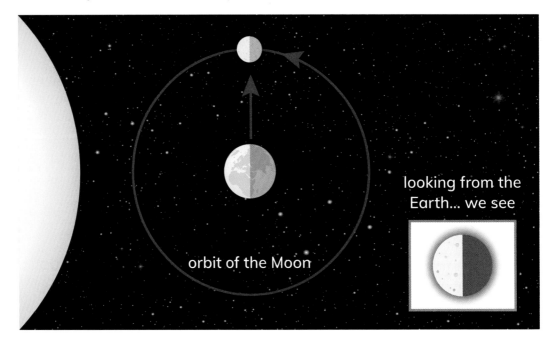

orbit of the Moon

looking from the Earth... we see

When the Moon is closer to the Sun than Earth, we see only
a little of the light side and lots of the dark side. This phase
is called a crescent moon.

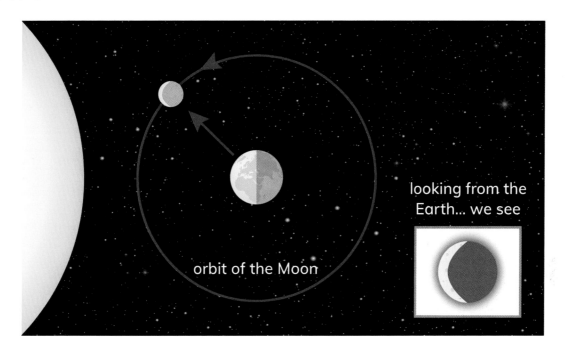

orbit of the Moon

looking from the
Earth... we see

When the light side of the Moon is getting bigger, we say the Moon
is waxing.

When it is getting smaller, we say the Moon is waning.

The Earth has a northern hemisphere
and a southern hemisphere.

The phases of the Moon look different from
the northern and southern hemispheres.

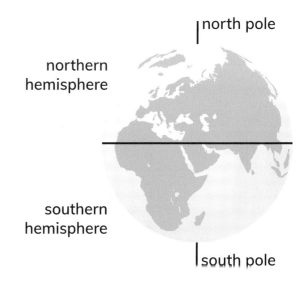

north pole

northern
hemisphere

southern
hemisphere

south pole

These are the eight phases of the Moon.

| new moon | waxing crescent | first quarter | waxing gibbous | full moon | waning gibbous | last quarter | waning crescent |

looking from the northern hemisphere

looking from the southern hemisphere

Think like a scientist 1

Modelling the phases of the Moon

You will need: a bright light and a white ball on a stick

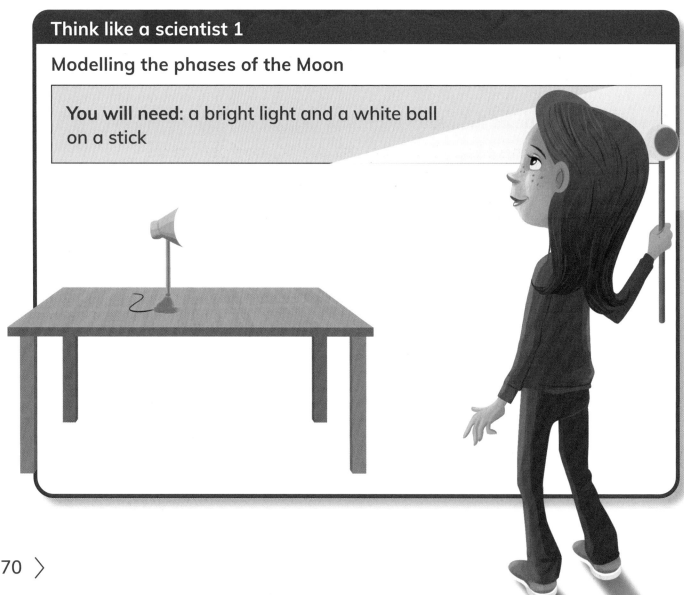

Continued

Sofia is modelling the phases of the Moon. As she turns, the ball makes a circle around her head. One side of the ball is always in the light. As she turns, she can see different amounts of the light side and dark side. In the picture she can see a waning crescent Moon.

Try doing this. Stand facing the light with the Moon in front of you. This is a new Moon. Turn slowly to your left and observe as the shadow on the Moon changes. Say the name of each phase as you see it.

How am I doing?

Help a friend to observe and name all the phases of the Moon.

Can they match the correct name to each phase?

Moonrise and Moonset

The Moon rises in the east, moves across the sky and sets in the west, just like the Sun. This is not because the Moon is moving. This is because the Earth is turning. We say it rotates. The Earth rotates once every day.

Because the Moon orbits the Earth, the time that the Moon rises and the time it sets is a bit later every day. So, the Moon can be up in the day or the night, but it is harder to see in the day.

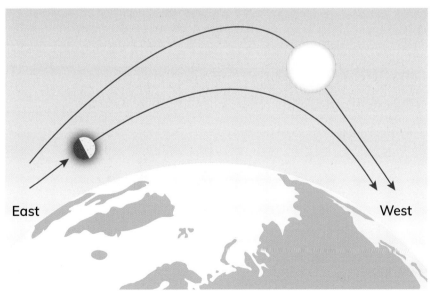

East   West

Think like a scientist 2

Making a Moon diary

You will need: a table to record your observations

Make a Moon diary by trying to observe and draw the Moon every day. Record your observations in a table like this.

Date	Monday 3rd February	Tuesday 4th February	Wednesday 5th February	Thursday 6th February	Friday 7th February	Saturday 8th February	Sunday 9th February
Observation	Waxing crescent	Waxing crescent	Cloudy	First quarter			
Rises: Sets:	4.20am 12.00pm	5.21am 12.50pm	6.10am 1.49pm	6.48am 2.55pm			

Find out what time the Moon rises and sets before trying to observe it. It might be on the other side of the Earth! If it is cloudy you may not be able to see the Moon. Draw it as often as you can.

What type of scientific enquiry did you use in this activity: research, pattern seeking, observing changes over time, fair testing or identification and classification?

Look what I can do!

☐ I can describe the phases of the Moon.

☐ I can describe why the Moon appears to move across the sky by describing the movement of the Earth and Moon.

☐ I can learn science from different types of model.

☐ I can record observations in a table.

Project: Research an astronaut

Astronauts needs to know lots about science.
They often do science investigations in space.

Yi So-yeon

A Korean astronaut who investigated how plants grow in space and how her own body changed.

Leroy Chiao

A Chinese American astronaut who investigated how gravity changes living things and materials.

Kalpana Chawla

An Indian astronaut who investigated how spiders build webs differently without gravity.

Rakesh Sharma

An Indian astronaut who made scientific observations of the Earth.

Wang Yaping

A Chinese astronaut who investigated medicine and gave a science lesson from space.

Continued

Make an astronaut poster.

Draw a picture of an astronaut and write some notes about them.

Use research to find out more about them.

Add what you find out to your poster.

Yi So-yeon

- South Korean
- Went to space April 8th 2008
- Grew plants in space
- investigated changes to her body

Check your progress

Talk about the answers to these questions with your class.

1   Arun and Zara are going to model the Earth and Moon.

Which of these objects would be best to use for the Earth?

Which would be best for the Moon?

Continued

2   A globe is a model of the Earth.

Why do we use models in science?

3   This diagram does not show things at the correct scale.

Which things are the wrong size in this diagram?

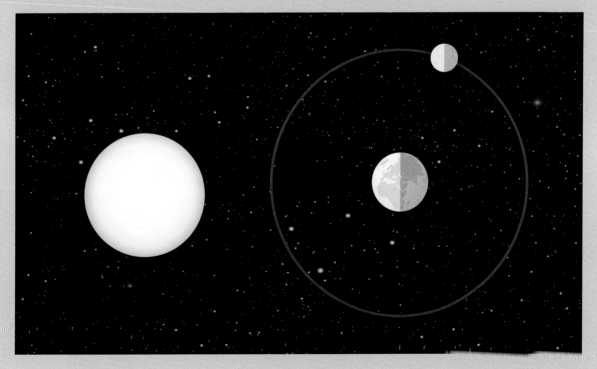

Continued

4 Marcus, Arun and Zara are explaining why the Moon has different phases.

Who is correct?

The shadow of the Earth falls on the Moon and makes different phases.

Sometimes the Sun lights up part of the Moon, sometimes it lights up all of the Moon.

The Sun lights up half of the Moon. We sometimes see lots of the light part and sometimes see lots of the dark part.

New science skills

Here are some of the scientific skills you will develop at Stage 3.

Measuring in standard units

Scientists like to use the same way of measuring so that everyone can compare their measurements. We call this using standard units. Standard units are used all around the world. We use them because they do not change and people everywhere can understand them.

When you measure length you use centimetres and metres. These are the standard units of length.

In science and mathematics we measure using standard units. Here are some examples:

time: seconds, minutes, hours, days

temperature: degrees centigrade

length: centimetres, metres

forces: newtons

To do science you need to learn to measure things correctly.

How to use a ruler

Put the zero on the ruler next to the end of the object.

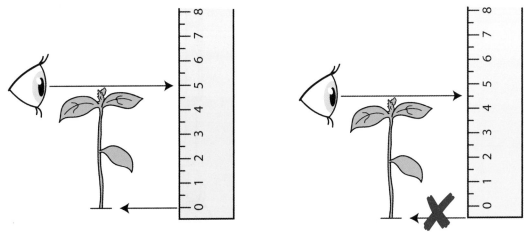

Put your eye level with the top of the object to read the scale.

Be careful. Often the zero is not at the end of the ruler.

How to use a thermometer to measure air temperature

Hold the thermometer at the top.

Put your eye level with the top of the liquid to read the scale.

Do not hold the bulb or the thermometer will measure the temperature of your fingers.

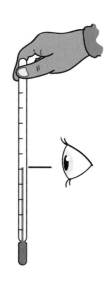

How to use a forcemeter

Turn the nut to make sure the forcemeter is set to zero.

Put the object on the forcemeter.

Put your eye level with the pointer and read the scale.

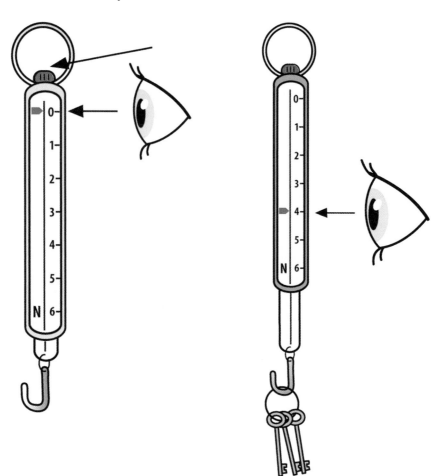

Drawing tables and using bar charts

Sofia and Marcus measure the growth of a seedling over five weeks.

They measure the seedling and add the result to a table. The table has space for each result. There is also a title at the top of the table.

It's day 5. The seedling is 9cm tall.

height	Week				
	1	2	3	4	5
	2cm	4cm	6cm	8cm	

These are the results shown in a table.

Table of results – how our seedling grew over five weeks					
	Weeks				
	1	2	3	4	5
Height of the seedling	2 cm	4 cm	6 cm	8 cm	9 cm

Now they draw a bar chart for these results.

On the left of the bar chart the numbers are in centimetres to show the different heights. They add the label 'Height (cm)' to show what the numbers mean.

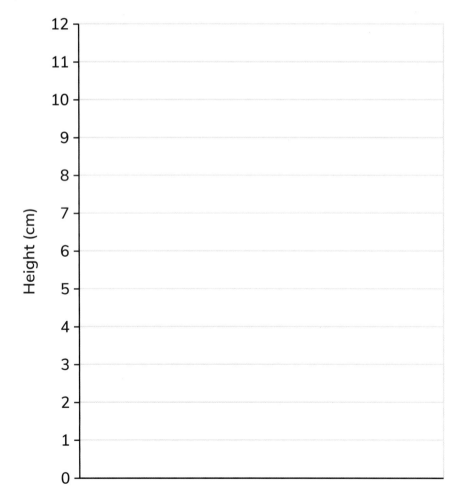

Along the bottom of the bar chart they add the numbers for five bars to show the five weeks. They add the label 'Weeks' to show what these numbers mean.

They then use a ruler to draw bars to show the results from the table.

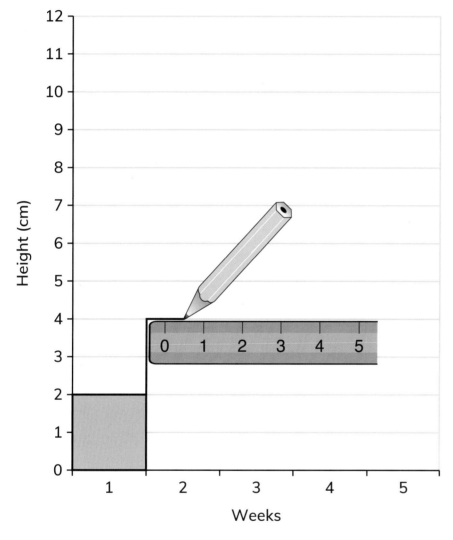

They draw the bars for all the results in the table.

They draw the bars touching one another but the bars do not have to touch.

They add a title for the bar chart to show what the chart is about.

Then they colour the bars to make them very clear.

The pattern of growth is clear on the bar chart.

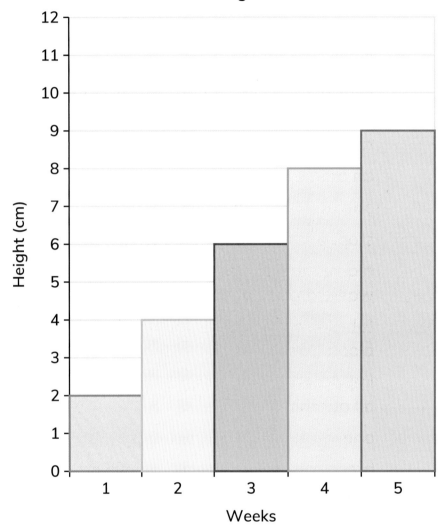

Bar chart showing growth of a seedling over 5 weeks

Glossary and index

Acknowledgements

The authors and publishers acknowledge the following sources of copyright material and are grateful for the permissions granted. While every effort has been made, it has not always been possible to identify the sources of all the material used, or to trace all copyright holders. If any omissions are brought to our notice, we will be happy to include the appropriate acknowledgements on reprinting.

Thanks to the following for permission to reproduce images:

Cover image by Pablo Gallego (Beehive Illustration); Inside *Unit 1*: Feellife/GI; Amir Mukhtar/GI; Lepro/GI; Tiziano Dal Betto/GI; Laszlo Selly/GI; Mint Images/GI; Princessdlaf/GI; Philippe Intraligi/GI; Lucas Joel Smeenge/GI; David Malan/GI; Science Photo Library/GI; Dave G Kelly/GI; Feellife/GI; Ed Reschke/GI; Cathlyn Melloan/GI; Sarayut Thaneerat/GI; Tonda/GI; Kalichka/GI; rbulthuis/GI; Cristian Bortes/GI; Borchee/GI; Halfpoint Images/GI; *Unit 2*: ER Productions Limited/GI; Charles D. Winters/Science Photo Library; Carol Yepes/GI; Juanmonino/GI; Jgalione/GI; Universal History Archive/GI; Kazi Salahuddin Razu/NurPhoto/GI; Bashir Osman's Photography/GI; Gosphotodesign/Gi; Wayne Hutchinson/Farm Images/Universal Images Group/GI; BrendanHunter/GI; Jasius/GI; LordRunar/GI; Stuart Cox/GI; Simon McGill/GI; Monty Rakusen/GI; Youst/GI; Tomekbudujedomek/GI; Photography by Mangiwau/GI; Monty Rakusen/GI; Alina Buzunova/GI; Richard Drury/GI; Jacobs Stock Photography Ltd/GI; *Unit 3*: Mordolff/GI; Klaus Vedfelt/GI; MamiEva/GI; JHVEPhoto/GI; Pickingpok/GI; Anyaberkut/GI; PhotoAlto/Anne-Sophie Bost/GI; Sally Anscombe/GI; Philippe Beyer/GI; John_Walker/GI; MediaProduction/GI; JodiJacobson/GI; Flashpop/GI; Adie Bush/GI; Pam Francis/GI; Karen Blumberg/GI; AleksandarNakic/GI; *Unit 4*: Thomas Demarczyk/GI; PeopleImages/GI; Sebastian Kaulitzki/GI; Gmint/GI; VW Pics/GI; Fernando Trabanco Fotografía/GI; George Doyle & Ciaran Griffin/GI; Viridis/GI; Cusoncom/GI; Antagain/GI; kuritafsheen/GI; Wayne R Bilenduke/GI; Thomas Pollin/GI; Peter Garner/GI; Daniel Trim Photography/GI; Wild Horizon/GI; Leonello Calvetti/GI; Naturfoto Honal/GI; Markrhiggins/GI; Jrroman/GI; Tiziano Dal Betto/GI; Wolfgang Kaehler/GI; HDH Lucas 2012/GI; ShutterStockStudio/Shutterstock; Ideeone/GI; Drmakkoy/GI; Phil Degginger/Carnegie Museum/Science Photo Library; *Unit 5*: Joe McBride/GI; Stefano Bianchetti/GI; Imagno/GI; Space Frontiers/GI; Tom Werner/GI; Pagadesign/GI; MamiGibbs/GI; SolStock/GI; Yobro10/GI; Jose Luis Pelaez Inc/GI; Prasert Sripodok/GI; Rubberball/Mike Kemp/GI; Georgy Rozov/GI; Miguel Navarro/GI; Gecko753/GI; JGI/Jamie Grill/GI; Haryigit/GI; CrailsheimStudio/GI; *Unit 6*: Mark Sutton/GI; Photovideostock/GI; Vitalij Cerepok/GI; Ktsdesign/Science Photo Library/GI; Mark Sutton/GI; Vitalij Cerepok/GI; ViewStock/GI; Ivo Peer/GI; Stocktrek Images/GI; NASA/GI; Len Collection/Alamy Stock Photo; Espen Norderud/GI; Sdart/GI; Alexander Nemenov/GI; Alexander Nemenov/GI; Apic/GI; Pallava Bagla/GI; Getty Images/GI; Junyyeung/GI; WilshireImages/GI.

Key GI=Getty Images